Available Light

Exile in Mexico

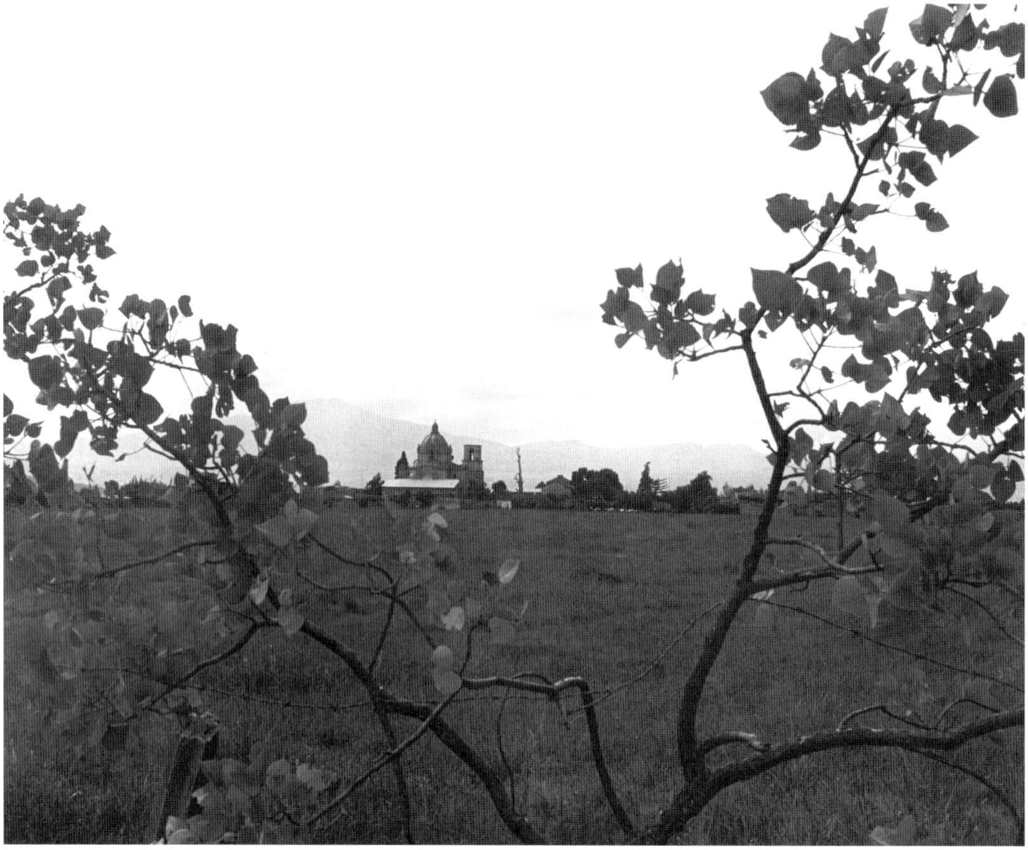

View of the village of Santa María del Guido, located in Michoacán, Mexico, near the city of Morelia. John Howard Griffin lived in this village during parts of 1960-1961.

Available Light

Exile in Mexico

Essays and Photographs by

John Howard Griffin

Edited and with an Introduction by

Robert Bonazzi

Foreword by Kathy Vargas

WingsPress

San Antonio, Texas

2008

This publication made possible in part by a generous grant from the City of San Antonio, Texas, Office of Cultural Affairs.

First Edition

ISBN-10: 0-916727-46-7
ISBN-13: 978-0-916727-46-8

Wings Press
627 E. Guenther
San Antonio, Texas 78210
Phone/fax: (210) 271-7805

On-line catalogue and ordering:
www.wingspress.com
All Wings Press titles are distributed to the trade by
Independent Publishers Group
www.ipgbook.com

Library of Congress Cataloging-in-Publication Data

Griffin, John Howard, 1920-1980.
Available light : exile in Mexico / essays and photographs by John Howard Griffin ; edited and with an introduction by Robert Bonazzi ; foreword by Kathy Vargas. -- 1st ed.
p. cm.
ISBN-13: 978-0-916727-46-8 (alk. paper)
ISBN-10: 0-916727-46-7 (alk. paper)
1. Portrait photography--Mexico--Tarasca Mountains. 2. Griffin, John Howard, 1920-1980. I. Bonazzi, Robert. II. Title.
TR680.G6978 2008
770.89'9796072--dc22

2008007178

Contents

Foreword

> I have no interest in the dramatic moment,
> but seek the moment that reveals the essential
> truths of an object or individual.
>
> – John Howard Griffin
> from "Notes on Photography" (p. 117)

When **photography,** the magic medium that draws with light, was first invented, it was embraced for its ability to tell the "truth." The fact that it could inform in a unique way – could be used to count the number of bricks in a wall, relate their tone and texture, and record the text written across them – became fused in the mind of its public and its practitioners with an ability to convey an unchanging reality. Soon, however, photographers with important truths to tell took the medium far beyond merely documenting the visible world. Banking on the public's trust in the veracity of photographs, they were able to shine a light into the dark recesses of man's unconcern, requiring a viewer's participation in his own salvation.

When John Howard Griffin went to Mexico to photograph, he had already walked that path from darkness to light. In relating his experiences as a Black man, an "Other" in an America on the verge of desegregation, with all its accompanying hysteria and panic, he'd dared to shine the glaring light of day on the darkest aspects of racism. Griffin's text forced his readers to choose sides: hatred or redemption. His strong sense of justice demanded that he speak, but his words evoked near-violent reactions within his own community.

Tumult and chaos followed the publication of the first "Journey into Shame" articles in the magazine *Sepia.* Griffin turned to Mexico and to photography for the kind of peace, grace, and order that allowed him simultaneously to craft his masterpiece. Working to perfect the technical requirements of picture making, he eloquently sought "to create the artifact that would involve the viewer." As with writing, he faced the challenge to feel his subject deeply, then to create a distance from that passion so that he might command the reason required for organizing the real world into art. Griffin understood well that photography's unique capacity to resemble reality must be carefully negotiated: "He must develop taste – so that what he selects (from all the possible elements to photograph in a subject) creates the illusion of reality rather than merely the greater clutter that is always involved in reality."

So what is this "distance" between reality and a meaningful illusion of reality for a man who has lived multiple lives? Griffin, besides living as a Black man, had also experienced a decade of blindness. Griffin worked well before the postmodernist's concern with "the gaze," but he was fully aware of an image maker's cultural biases in picturing "the Other." How does one such as Griffin see, now that he has become hyper-conscious of being gazed upon and discarded or despised? How does he photograph – he who, married to social justice, could never eye his fellow humans with the same disdain he'd encountered when he was in another's skin?

The answer is in each work presented, and in each word used to assess and justify his photos. Particularly poignant is the photograph of a Tarascan woman walking down the street, her basket on her arm (p. 15). This image encapsulates Griffin's great desire in committing the Tarascans to film: "And in the framework of the universal, to capture something of these other individualizing elements."

Using Barthes' method of analysis, the "studium" places the woman within the context of her time and place, her culture and her community; it also locates us as viewers: in our individual known worlds, separate from her and gazing. Here again is that distance, yet one filled with both respect and a kind of joy: the photographer's respect for her dignity and his joy in seeing a strong woman looking back. The "punctum" is that she is secure in her stride, her bare feet about to step out of the frame. This woman is not contained by the "reality" presented in the photo. She knows that this is only 1/125th of a second of her time and that she will continue her life somewhere beyond the picture's edges. Her steady gaze is level with that of the photographer and so she looks us in the eye. She has also seen "the Other." This makes equals of us all – whomever has looked on this silver surface in years past or will see it for years to come – without waiting to see whether or not equality is possible. The maker of this artifact of witness has already acknowledged that equality, and thus makes us accomplices in divine grace.

This is Griffin's great gift: that he does not doubt *our* humanity. That he truly feels, as did so many of the great social documentary photographers, that this magic medium can and "must soften in its little way, even for only a few seconds, the great callous that lies on the hearts of so many."

– Kathy Vargas

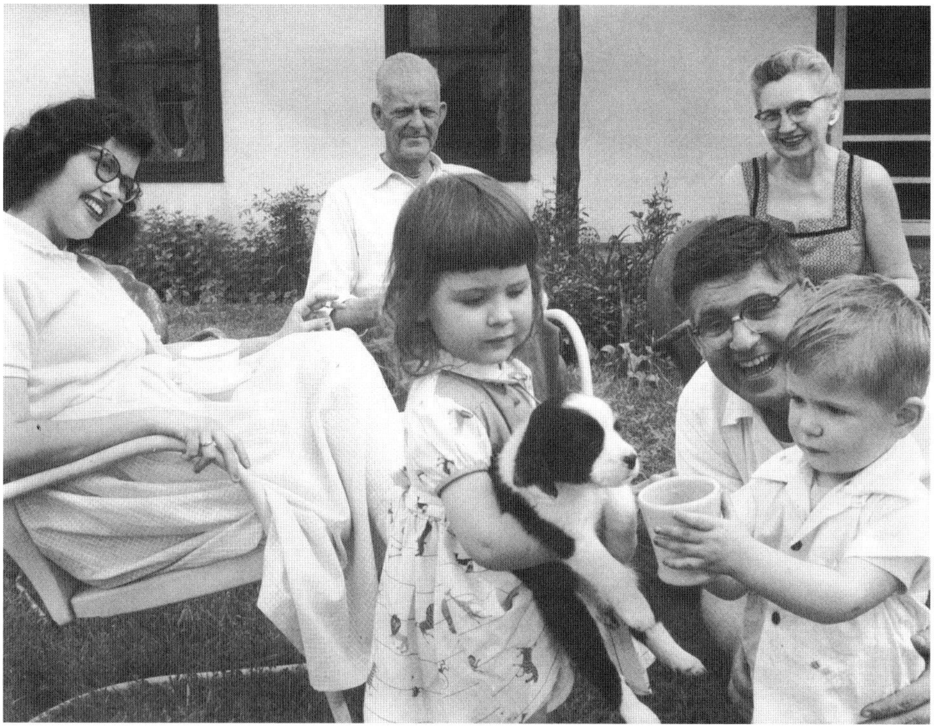

The extended Griffin family during happier times in Mansfield, Texas, before their move to Mexico. From left to right in background: Elizabeth, wife of John Howard Griffin; Jack Griffin, his father and Lena Griffin, his mother. In foreground: Griffin children Susan and Johnny, offering a cup to their puppy, to the delight of their father, John Howard Griffin, and everyone else. This photograph was taken by Shel Hershorn, but not included in a series on Griffin that Hershorn made for *Life* magazine in 1958; reproduced with permission.

Exile in Mexico

An Introduction

Robert Bonazzi

From Texas to Mexico

After **returning** from a six week journey through the Deep South disguised as a "Negro" in 1959, an experience which would become the classic, *Black Like Me* in 1961, John Howard Griffin prepared to move his young family and elderly parents to Morelia, Mexico to avoid the racist threats they were receiving from residents in their hometown of Mansfield, Texas.

"We prepare to leave for Mexico," Griffin wrote in his *Journal*, on August 4, 1960, "after 13 years here in this barn studio, and I try to sort my books – books gathered over the past 20 years of my life. Strange to go back over them, to dig them out and decide what to give, what to sell, what to keep."

Griffin examined, with nostalgic selectivity, certain books that had been packed away since 1949, when he had returned from France, then totally blind. He regained his sight in January of 1957. This entry, written on the threshold of the long-delayed departure for Mexico to reunite with his family, who had flown ahead a few weeks before, floats to other worlds and times.

> The sun scorches the countryside and overpowers the best efforts of an old, old fan that once cooled my Grandfather's store in South Dallas.
>
> Things forgotten, things not seen in years or, again, many that I got while I was blind and never saw until I went through storage boxes today. They range from magnificent volumes, like the *Paléographie Musicale* from Solesmes, to our little two franc school volumes of Molière and Hugo. All represent periods of momentary enthusiasm that flared and then cooled to affection that remains to this day. Each was once held between my hands with that excitement nothing else can quite parallel.
>
> I find an old and worn copy of another French book, and it brings back the incidents long dead in my memory – the cluttered second-hand bookshop near the Cathedral of Tours. The purchase

> for little or nothing, the excitement then of hurrying to my room, up darkened steps, and finally sitting in a chair near the dormer windows and opening the world. . . .The experience of taking out and examining these beautiful things becomes almost unbearable – the evocations are fresh, stripped to their essences, and the essences were good, indeed terribly good for all of it was discovery, marvel, delight.

Only his grandfather's fan moved the air on that sun-scorched day which reached 105 degrees. Griffin did not mention it here, but it was his maternal grandfather, Samuel Clements Young, who had introduced him to books. Every night, the old man had read from a set of *The Harvard Classics,* passing them on volume by volume to his grandson, until finally bequeathing the entire set to the future author.

The "magnificent volumes" of the *Paléographie Musical,* bound scores of Gregorian Chant, had been brought over from the Abbey of St. Pierre de Solesmes, where Griffin had studied music with the Benedictine monks. These are leather-bound collections with texts in Latin, title pages and prefaces in French, and printed on heavy, semi-gloss stock with gold-leafed edges. According to the dates written on the inside of the cheap French-language paperbacks of Molière and Hugo, those had been purchased in 1936, at the beginning of his education at the Lycée Descartes in Tours.

While it had been the Gestapo that drove Griffin (then a member of the French underground resistance) out of Tours in 1939, he was being forced from Mansfield by local racists. The family would leave before Griffin, who stayed on to finish chores. For him, the departure was bittersweet and no more so than on this day, as he reminisced about other places he had been forced to abandon. And that was not all.

That night he wrote to his mentor, French philosopher Jacques Maritain, from whom he had received a distressing letter that day about his wife Raïssa's illness. "Late at night – the fan fights the tremendously heavy heat and puts a hum into the Bach. I read and try to answer Maritain's letter, so full of pain."

> Above all, know that you are not alone, that everywhere in the world you are loved, not only because you are Jacques and Raïssa

Official portrait of the French philosopher, Jacques Maritain, taken by Griffin, summer, 1964. The portrait appeared in periodicals worldwide, as well as in the book by Griffin, *Jacques Maritain: Homage in Words and Pictures* (1974).

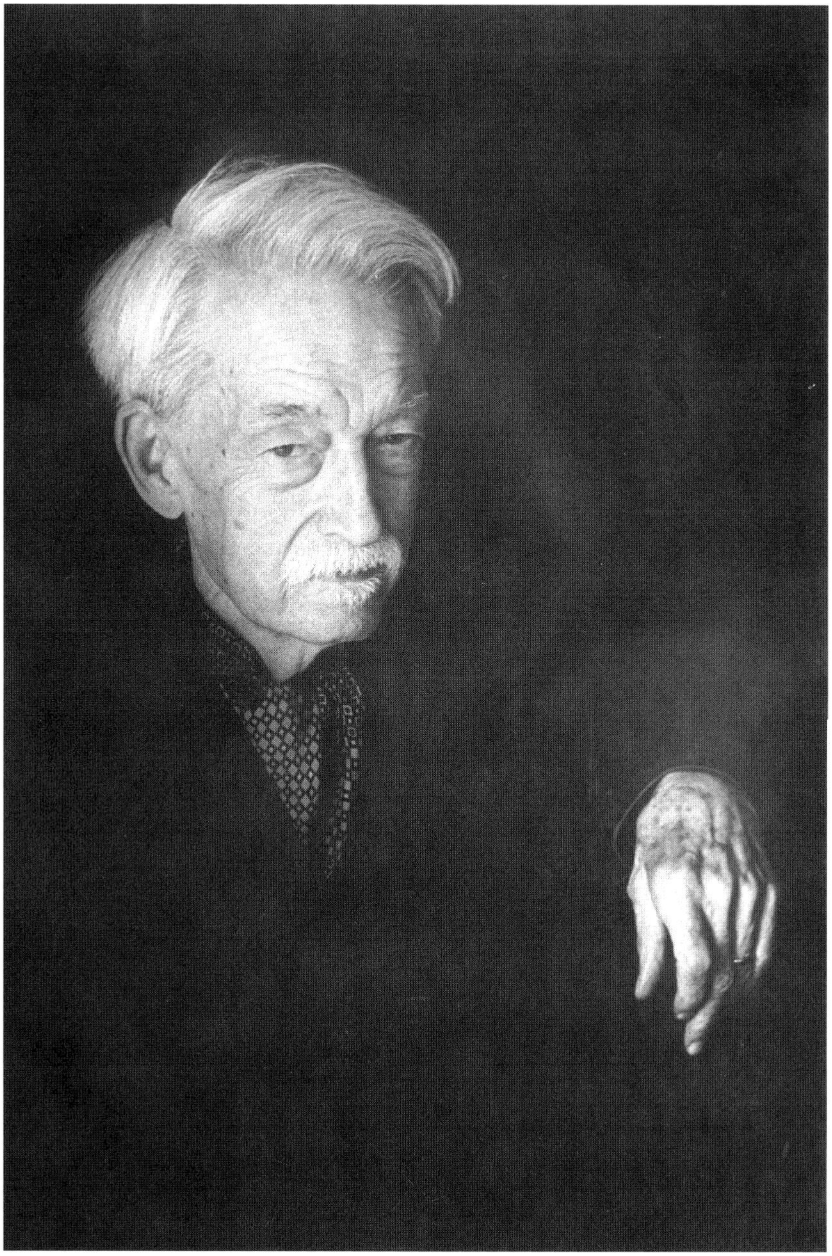

> Maritain, the philosopher and poet, but because you are you. It's strange, simple, a peasant blushes in his clumsiness while trying to write a 'love letter' to the great poet-philosopher and the great philosopher-poet. But it's that way . . . and since long ago. How to say thank-you to two people who have (after St. Thomas) been the greatest formative influence since your adolescence? How many others are spiritually your children in this sense? Many more than you imagine. How many others, ordinary types like myself, have taken fire thanks to you, and have worked in the "Thomist" liberation you have procured for them? I know a number – and authentic ones – who have taken this lamp, lighted by you, and have gone into the shadows to illuminate, by their art or their science, the obscure corners of the world.

He wrote Father J. Stanley Murphy to let him know of Maritain's "very distressing" letter. Father Stan, as everyone called him, was also a mentor and sometime confessor of Griffin's. The Basilian priest at Assumption College in Windsor, Ontario, had known the Maritains since 1942, when Jacques received the Christian Culture Award, a series Murphy had initiated in 1941.

> Jacques speaks of Raïssa's falling ill in Paris; better now but with a long and dolorous convalescence ahead of her. He has spoken repeatedly of the hell of his life since Vera's death [Raïssa's sister], without specifying. . . . Lord, when you think of what this man has given the world; what some poor beggar like myself owes him in formation, and then to be impotent to do anything to make things easier for them.

Griffin also told Father Stan that he had worked "harder than ever in my life" on the two versions of his journey as a disguised Black man traveling through the Deep South, "and with more love and a greater feeling of desolation than ever." This was the last letter he wrote to any of his friends until reaching Mexico.

On August 9, he made his last *Journal* entry from the studio. The first half is a jubilant description of a sudden rain storm "after weeks of drought, all the more wondrous because nothing led us to expect it."

However, after the mail arrived that day, nerves once again were frayed. "Dad brought the mail, with that long-suffering expression of patience on his face, of pain and anguish; another no-return address letter, another threat, another promise. I tore it open and read it. The writer tells me 'they' have definitely set the date for August 15. 'So fuck your wife good, you half-nigger bastard. After August 15 you won't have balls or peter. Your time is up. You are marked.'"

He stuffed the letter in a pocket and showed it to no one. However, his father was able to read the postcard that had arrived with the mail. Scrawled in pencil was the simple message: "August 15 is the date." Griffin's mother walked into the room and responded to "the mournful, the terrible glance" of her husband's face. Even without having read it, she blurted out: "Well, let's go now. Let's pack up and drive away."

Six days later, on August 13, Lena and Jack Griffin left Mansfield and drove to Taos, New Mexico, to spend a few days with old family friends, Sally and Hannah Gillespie. From there they would travel on to Mexico to meet their son's family.

On August 15, Elizabeth and the three children flew to Mexico City. They were met there by Robert Ellis, a painter the Griffins had known since 1953, and his wife, Rosa, a native of Mexico. After more than three hours in customs, a kindly clerk intervened, allowing the Ellises (who were bilingual) to enter the glassed-encased area. Everything was settled quickly and the weary Texas family was waved through. Robert Ellis drove them 45 miles to Toluca, to the home of Rosa's family, where they met the couple's two-year-old daughter, Erendira, for the first time.

Griffin stayed on alone in Mansfield through August 15, to challenge the racists with their deadline, but no violence occurred. He sold the last of his parents' furniture and traded his English Ford in on a 1960 Corvair, figuring that since Chevrolet had plants in Mexico, parts for it would be easier to find.

Early on the morning of August 18, Griffin loaded the car with everything he could squeeze into it. Elizabeth had taken six large suitcases containing their clothes. He loaded the photography equipment, a record player and boxes of albums, a recorder and tapes, and enough cookware and dishes and utensils to begin a new life. It was his intention to relocate permanently in Santa María del Guido, a little village on a mountainside overlooking Morelia. The plan was to remodel an old hacienda owned by his brother, Edgar, and to send the children to a French lycée in Morelia. Meanwhile, he was packed to capacity, with only a tunnel between the rear-view mirror and the back windshield and, with a touch of unplanned humor, an ironing board thrusting nearly halfway out the passenger window.

He described his departure after he had arrived in Mexico. "I began again to keep this *Journal* after a long silence. I, who wanted so much to leave the horrors of this past experience, to come to Mexico, left one morning with the car loaded. Instead of relief and joy, I experienced an immense, almost pathological sadness. I drove out of Mansfield where I have lived 13 years and no one said good-bye or good luck. Most were invisible, but those on the streets simply stared after me, convinced I have no doubt that they had driven the bastard away."

Griffin drove southwest across the Staked Plains region of Texas, which he had written about in *Land of the High Sky* a few years before. "A tremendous heaviness filled me and I could not shake it." He laid over in an El Paso motel, after a long, hot day and 450 miles. The next morning he drove to a border check, passed through customs, and crossed the bridge over the Rio Grande into Mexico. Late that night he drove around the sprawling metropolis of Mexico City, and continued west to Toluca. He arrived at the home of Rosa Ellis' family about four in the morning, on August 20. The house was dark and everyone was asleep. Robert Ellis responded quickly to the knock at the door. The two old friends greeted each other as "compadre," in the traditional manner they had adopted in the early 1950s. The painter knew how tired Griffin must be, because Ellis had made countless trips to Mexico from his Texas birthplace of Jacksboro (about 50 miles northwest of Mansfield).

On the morning of August 21, the Griffins and Ellises set out in a caravan across the mountains west toward Michoacán. After a grinding eight-hour day through 200 miles of winding roads, they arrived in Morelia and took rooms in a downtown hotel. Within a few days, Griffin had rented a furnished apartment in the mountain village. Santa María del Guido would be their new home in Mexico. Once the Griffins had settled in, the Ellises returned to their home in Valle de Bravo.

Elizabeth Griffin on the balcony of the only hotel in Santa María (1960). Like most of the photographs by Griffin in this book, the image appears for the first time in print.

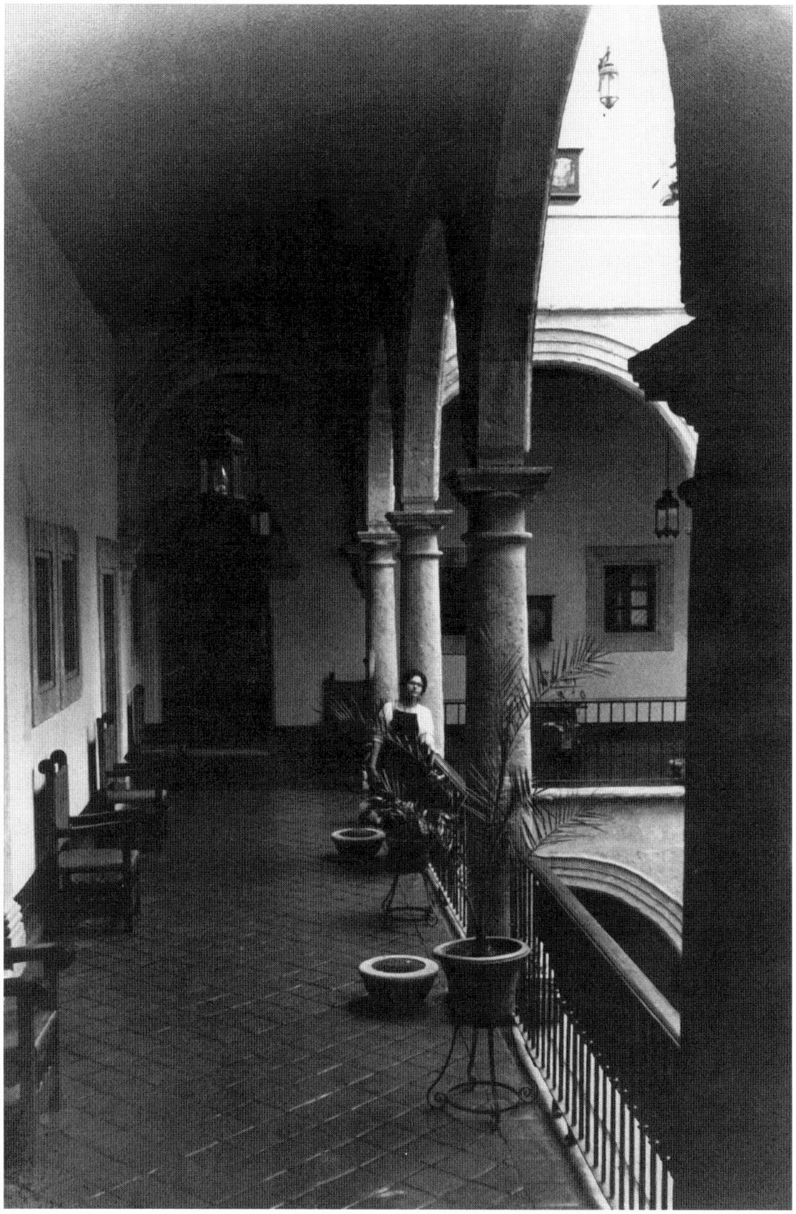

For the remainder of August and all of September, they lived in an apartment across the street from the Villa Montana Restaurant. Early during their stay, they became well acquainted with the owner of the restaurant, Ramón Coté, and the delicious traditional cuisine he offered.

But they also cooked in the apartment kitchen, shopped at the local market, and began to speak Spanish, while learning the terrain of the charming little village. For the first time ever, Elizabeth had a maid and this freed her to take the children to market, while Griffin oversaw the remodeling of Edgar's hacienda.

One evening in September, as Griffin was playing a Mozart record, he heard a different Mozart piece singing through the thin wall separating their apartment from the one next door. Griffin knocked on that door and invited the couple for coffee. He was astonished to discover Luis Berbér, conductor of *Los Niños Cantores de Morelia* (known worldwide as "The Singing Boys of Mexico"), and his wife, Wilenne, a native of Fort Worth, close to Mansfield. This chance meeting began a lasting friendship.

A few days later, they met Barbara and Don Shoemaker, also Americans in Mexico, who owned a prosperous furniture shop in the village. Through the Shoemakers and Berbérs, the new family became known and trusted in the village. Meanwhile, Griffin's parents had arrived from New Mexico, immediately renting the guest house at the Denton Estate, owned by wealthy Americans then in Europe. The Griffin family moved into the main house. "All of us are well," he wrote in his *Journal,* "we live in the Denton home, with high stone walls around a large grounds filled with flowers – a splendid and cheerful home to occupy while we wait for Edgar's house to be finished. I work in the guest room, separated from the main house by a patio. It is a typical native room with red brick floors, white adobe walls, a corner fireplace, windows looking out to the mountains. The room has a private bath which I have turned into a darkroom. I have lost myself in film work."

The Artist in Exile

During the autumn of 1960, Griffin finally settled into a productive cycle of writing, photography and research at the Denton house. He realized that the fears and frustrations of the Mansfield aftermath to his Deep South journey had left him in a state of depression and that all the moving had been dislocating. "I knew I was reacting dangerously and sought to counter it, but the effects went too deep and it has taken me almost two months to regain sufficient voice to put anything down on paper." Now that he was secure in the new studio and darkroom, the emotional wounds had healed and he had gained a certain aesthetic distance from his experiment. His task became a matter of reshaping the story he had written about in the *Sepia* magazine series, "Journey Into Shame," into the book that would become *Black Like Me.* Before writing again, he had immersed himself in every aspect of photography, aiming for a higher level of technical control. "Thank God," he said that "there was this absorption in something new."

This Mexico period would mark his breakthrough as a visual artist. Simultaneously, it also initiated a deep understanding of the creative harmony achievable in combining photography and writing. He would develop this fresh vision over the entire span of his exile, from September 1960 to May 1961. He outlined the goal in his *Journal:*

> The desire to do my own photography, and in some way to combine it with my writing, would not leave me. I wanted to see if my eye could capture the particular modality that had haunted me in my loss of sight, and again in my recovery of sight: To catch humanity not in its drama so much as its truth, its intelligence.

When Griffin had been without sight between 1946-1957, he felt that he could peer into the heart of a person, that he could sense a truth he could not see with his eyes. He heard it in the naked tone of their unguarded voices. He was able to perceive in a way as mysterious as it was objective, like a lens that could “see without partiality,” a truth that the sighted overlooked.

In “Notes on Photography,” a typescript composed at the Denton house, Griffin searched for a way to clarify what might obscure his eye to what the lens revealed: To see what was really there, rather than being trapped once again in the unconscious phenomenon of selective inattention. He believed that “the personal vision of the photographer” – not the acuity of eyesight but one’s vision of essences – “can and does make the originality of his work.”

> If his vision is purely visual, then he can only produce images. If his vision is philosophical, then the work will take on a density of concept that opens the door to originality even in the most banal shots.
>
> He must develop taste – so that what he selects (from all the possible elements to photograph in a subject) creates the illusion of reality rather than merely the greater clutter that is always involved in reality. He must go through great complexity, for every image, every communication is immensely complex, in order to arrive at simplicity – in order to make his vision speak his own language.

His photographic approach to this problem of perceiving what is there – instead of substituting a stereotype or projecting one’s own subjectivity upon the subject – was evolving as “something more than the ‘know your subject’ conventionality.”

> I looked upon my neighbors, the Tarascans, and sought those elements in their culture that were universal to all men, and then sought those elements that were special to their ancient and beautiful culture: qualities of tenderness and dignity toward children; extreme fidelity to friendship; generosity and simplicity. And in the framework of the universal, to capture something of these other individualizing elements.

The Purépecha tribe, ancestors of the native people we know as the Tarascans, came to prominence in western Mexico during the 13th century. It is not known from where this once-nomadic tribe originated or exactly when they migrated to the region of Michoácan (which means "the place of fish"). Their civilization was nearly equal in size to the Aztec empire, and they were the only people in Mexico *not* to be conquered by the Aztecs. The Tarascan empire achieved its zenith just before the arrival of the Spanish, early in the 16th century. The name "Tarascan" was given to the Purépeches by the Spaniards, meaning "son-in-law" (*tarasco* in Purépecha). To avoid war, the Tarascans offered the daughters of the court to the conquistadors as gifts of friendship. Since the Spaniards heard this word constantly, they mistook it for the name of the tribe. The Spanish chroniclers had called the Tarascans "the most beautiful of the Mexican Indians." Griffin described them as "aristocratic, beautiful, and aloof."

He discovered universality in the native rituals, with its curiously rich mixture of indigenous and Catholic influences. He traveled to the island of Janitzio to photograph the Day of the Dead, the Tarascan version of Mexico's All Soul's Day, in November of 1960 ("The Watch of the Dead"); later he also ventured to witness the events of Holy Week in Tzintzuntzan in 1961 ("Passion at Tzintzuntzan").

Besides these trips, he continued practicing with the camera and its lenses, the Leitz enlarger and darkroom chemicals; and he walked the countryside to study light meter readings in relation to film-speed and exposures. He made a dedicated effort to meet the Tarascans, hoping they would be less uncomfortable with the uncased camera at his side.

"The Tarascans, however, until one knows them," he noticed, "are extremely reluctant to be photographed." But he found ways to take photographs at a distance. The culture and landscape "offered endless wealth to the photographer in material." Yet his essential question remained: How to select the discreet image from the obvious possibilities? He did not take rapid-fire pictures, did "not shoot promiscuously," since overcoming an early inclination to shoot too much film. His visual images were like entries in his *Journal* – he would ruminate and search out what was there, he would be patient, he would wait. Eventually, those images and words were revisited by a different perspective, which would be developed in the darkroom or on the typewriter.

Griffin approached photography as he had writing – going his own way, never greatly influenced by the work of others. During a decade of physical blindness, he did not allow himself to be limited by conventional social expectations; rather, he had accomplished what the sightless were not supposed to accomplish. Everything was a matter of personal ethics, experiment, and asking why not. Just as he had based his novels on musical forms, he related the challenges of photography to what he had learned from writing fiction. Always, he sought out the mysterious, as he writes in "Notes on Photography":

> If I sought light, composition, expression – nevertheless I was aiming at something else, something the novelist must deal with – the expression of the basically inexpressible. In other words, a combination of elements that would produce the resonances in the viewer that I wanted him to have; works that would do something to the viewer rather than merely please the eye."

It was an artistic and philosophical challenge for Griffin. Philosophical in that it involved ethics, aesthetics and metaphysics, once study and practice had brought the technical skills to a natural fluency. He parallels the pursuit of photography with that of writing, as arts of "selectivity" in his "Notes on Photography":

> I realized that the photographer often errs when he photographs a thing that has great subjective importance, thinking it will strike the viewer with the same overtones. The point of challenge is to analyze this, and to set about deliberately, with technique and imagination, to create the artifact that would involve the viewer. This is also the novelist's constant challenge; it is the reason why the definition of art as "selectivity" is such a valid one.

That is, selecting and reshaping what is real, actually there in the images or the words. Art attempts to transform the essence of reality into an essential artifact. The artist must be consciously in control of the creative process, aware of its essences, before imagination can be tapped. In the case of the photographer's work, "it must express what he wants to express, it must be deliberate

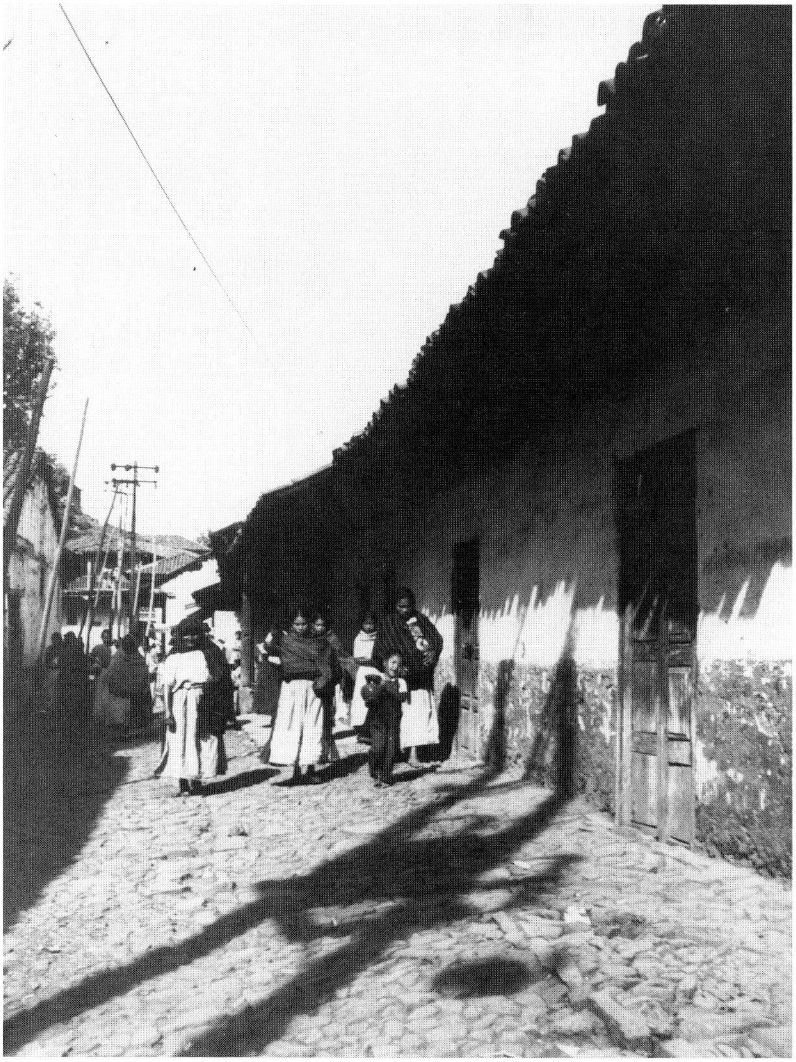

Tarascan women and children walking on one of the stone streets of the village.

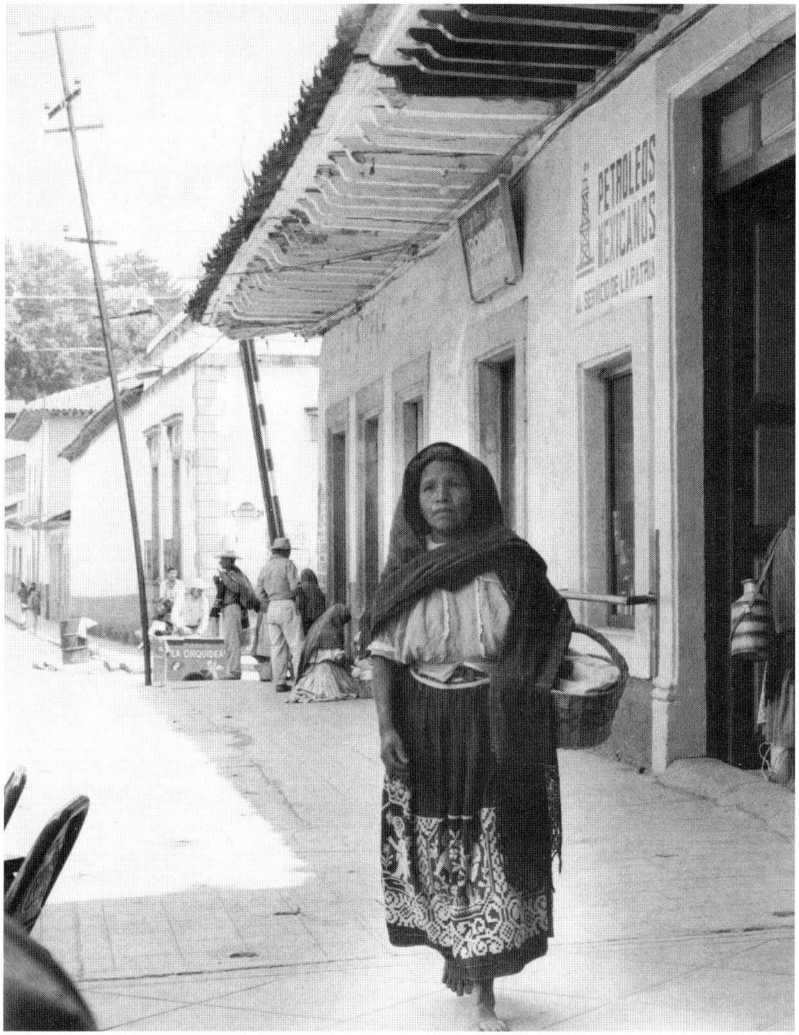

Tarascan woman with basket doing her shopping in the village.

and he must choose the means of making it so," Griffin writes in "Notes on Photography."

> The photographer must master the art of developing and printing, which are highly individual techniques that no one else can do for him, in order to bring out exactly his vision. He must feel, after the mastery of technique is out of the way, a continuously greater freedom to stretch his medium and his belief in its capabilities.

Griffin's vision of combining photography and writing came into sharp focus when he witnessed the Day of the Dead ritual in early November of 1960. On the second day of that month, he recorded the experience in his *Journal.*

> I have returned this morning from the Island of Janitzio, a small, legend-rich Tarascan island that rises up out of Lake Patzcuaro. There, All Soul's Day is celebrated by a night-watch at the cemetery, in the belief that the dead return to visit their living – a mixture of pagan and Catholic ritual, dating from some aboriginal past and somehow intermingled with the Catholic faith. It is not a sad occasion, but a quiet one, a tender one to those who believe that their dead return to visit with them – and all more or less hold this belief.

This ritual challenged his technical skills as a photographer. The result was a single folio of images, which he arranged on matte boards as *Return of the Spirit*. In the images from Janitzio and the personal essay about attending the ritual, there is a natural integration of senses in a near-silent hush of absorption. The images are simple, lucid, reverent. They resonate without shouting. The tone of the essay matches the awe of the visual experience – a brief narrative that does not call attention to is own voice.

Griffin had to obtain official clearance to photograph the ritual. He was informed that the request would only be considered if he met the strict prohibition on the use of flash equipment. He assured them that he would photograph discretely and without any supplementary lighting. In any case, he was told that the islanders would have the final say; they had grown weary of tourists with flash cameras, liquor, and poor manners.

When he arrived at the docks, he saw boatloads of visitors on the lake heading toward the island, and he doubted that he would be allowed to go. But he learned that the orders against visitors had been rescinded. "Local police let us pass, one by one after making certain we did not carry flash equipment or liquor and with a polite admonition that we make ourselves no more obnoxious than necessary," Griffin writes. He crossed over, climbed the "steep cobblestone street toward the church halfway up the hill in the last dim light of dusk," and reaching it, pushed open the heavy doors of the church. Everything was set out to be blessed – long-burning candles, bouquets of flowers, fresh-baked bread. Everything was blessed for the living spirit of the beloved dead. "Shawled women and children and hatless men knelt," Griffin writes, "dark masses in the flickering light, absorbing the fresh odor of incense."

After a pleasant talk with a priest, who advised him to eat heartily before going up to the site, he had a meal of fresh fish. Then, in the chilled darkness, he walked up the side of the mountain to the *panteón* – "a flat tabletop of perhaps two acres bounded on one side by the sheer rise of a cliff and on the other by a low wall over which we looked down on the lake below." He entered through "a high stone arch topped by a cross," which he photographed. There were no grave markers or mounds at the burial sites. Candles by the thousands and several wood fires illuminated the cliff. Those parents, awaiting the spirits of their children, spread out toys and mangoes on colorful blankets. He moved about slowly, quietly, "another mere shadow in the candlelit night." He was not rebuffed. "The Tarascans, a people of the greatest natural dignity and beauty, asked only that we not openly intrude."

Suddenly there was a garish flash of a camera. A wave of murmuring protest followed as the man set off another flashbulb. The man was escorted away and Griffin slipped his camera back in its case. He took no more pictures for an hour, until the mood became less strained, returning to its previous serenity. About ten o'clock the night turned colder. He sat on the ground near an elderly woman, whose face was highlighted by the tall candles. "Do you want to photograph me?" she asked in Spanish. He had noticed the magical glow on her face, so meditative, austere. "May I?" he asked and she agreed. He shot three frames and thanked her.

By midnight, most of the visitors were driven away by the increasing cold. Griffin met a Mexican anthropologist and his wife, who gave him a cup of coffee from their thermos. They sat on a stone bench at the edge of the *panteón*, discussing the ritual and Griffin's attempt to photograph it without flash equipment. As he explained, his teeth began to chatter and his hands became so numb he was barely able to use the camera. All around them, small children were being wrapped in blankets and moved near the small fires. Most of the children slept, but those who remained awake did not utter a complaint. About two that morning, "the quiet murmur of conversations hushed as a woman's sobbing shocked the atmosphere," but she went quickly silent.

Just before dawn, the priest arrived to celebrate Mass. No one moved from their places and all were attentive to the sacrament. After Mass dawn emerged and the islanders silently disappeared from the deserted *panteón*.

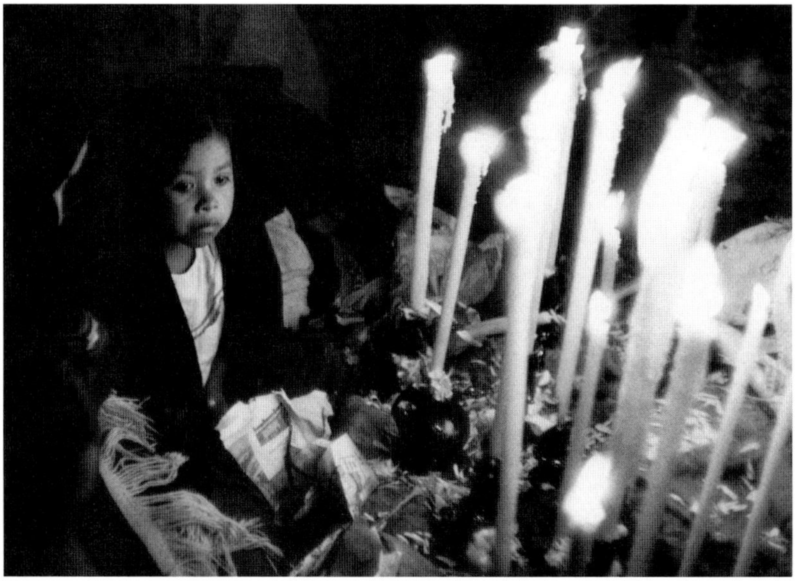

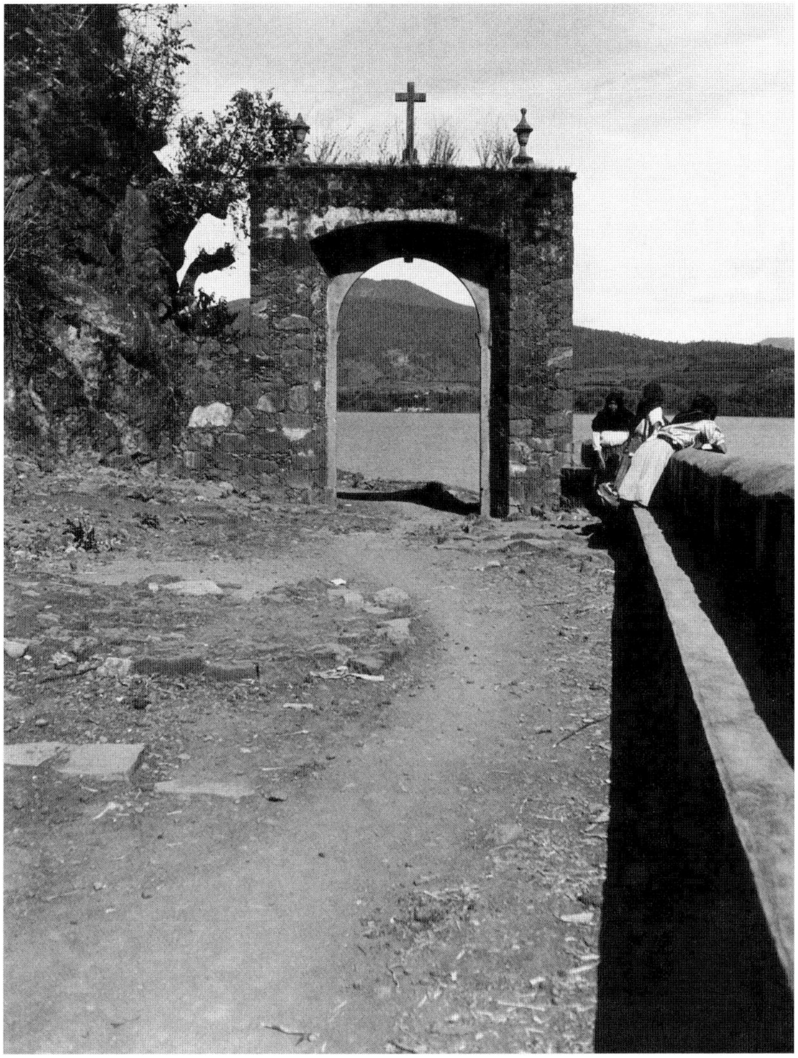

Tarascan women at the entrance to the panteón on the afternoon before that night's celebration of Watch of the Dead ritual, which takes place annually on All Souls Eve on the island village of Janitzio in Lake Patzcuaro.

Deeper Rhythms of Work

"Life here settles into the deeper rhythms of work," wrote Griffin in a letter to Father Stan Murphy, on November 7, 1960. He had just completed the research for an article on the Black Man and Catholicism – a piece that would be published as "Racist Sins of Christians" in the most popular Catholic magazine of the day, *The Sign,* in 1963.

> It took a good deal of research, and the material is so vast I could not begin to cover it properly in 5000 words. At least it made me proud of the Church if ashamed of many of our fellow Catholics who, in their desire to possess both God and their prejudices, reek of the child in tantrum.
>
> How nice it is to write from such a place. The great silence, the immense views on a sunlit day – the noises of my children in other rooms, my feeling of pride as I went back into the history of the Church and saw how uncompromisingly, how courageously, She has always pronounced herself in these matters of racism (even here among the Tarascans). Most of all, the sense of immense privilege that this might be the means of clarifying someone's doubts – of encouraging one poor soul to see through the fog of our imperfections as Catholics and blunderers to the true value of the Faith, and perhaps to go that way himself and find there what we know is there . . . . How many have we defrauded with the Faith through our obtuseness? It is staggering when one goes into it. For once though, the situation is optimistic – even a poor Catholic cannot stomach too much injustice, cannot deliberately live in grave sin for long.

Griffin closed with a request for the priest's prayers and a brief report on how the family was doing so well in Mexico and happy to be away from the racists back home. "Pray that we will be allowed to remain here and work for eternity, rather than run and get ourselves mixed up in the mess again."

A week later, Griffin received an Aerogramme from Father Stan, breaking the sad news that Raïssa Maritain had died on November 4. Griffin wrote immediately to Jacques Maritain and let mutual friends know the news in several other letters.

Nonetheless, the continual cycle of writing and photography continued apace. Eight of the Tarascan photographs were accepted for publication by the agency representing the boys choir, and he was also asked to write an essay for what would become a booklet, *The Singing Boys of Mexico,* in 1962. It would be the only context in which more than a few of his Tarascan photographs would appear in print.

In late November, he wrote letters to Father Stan and Decherd Turner, an old friend who would become Griffin's first literary executor. Turner had sent Griffin the journal of the Perkins School of Theology (of Southern Methodist University). "Your article was particularly appealing to me," he wrote of Turner's introduction, "and valid and very good and tough – the way you are when you are best . . . a nice tone of affection that makes the observations shine right, even when they are most critical." Also he mentions a telegram received from the National Council of Negro Women, announcing that he had won their annual award for the *Sepia* series. "I am to fly to Los Angeles for a press conference and to receive the award or whatever one does."

In his letter to Father Stan, he asked for prayers that he would "have some shred of wisdom in all this." He also thanked the priest for inviting Luis Berbér and the choir to perform at the program of the 1961 Christian Culture Series in Windsor, Ontario. A long *Journal* entry for November 26, outlined other recent activities.

Adelle Jackson, editor of *Sepia,* sent an article by Carl Rowan, "Are Negroes Ready for Equality?" (published in the *Saturday Evening Post*). Griffin read it, "astonished at the obtuseness of the title question. Man is ready for equality by the very fact of his birth." Mrs. Jackson asked him to write a response for *Sepia.* Since the whole thesis of any man's 'readiness for equality' is off-key, it will not be difficult to do."

Griffin's response to the syndicated Black journalist, who was a political conservative, was published in the March 1961 issue of *Sepia,* and the dialogue caused controversy in the pages of subsequent issues. In general, Black

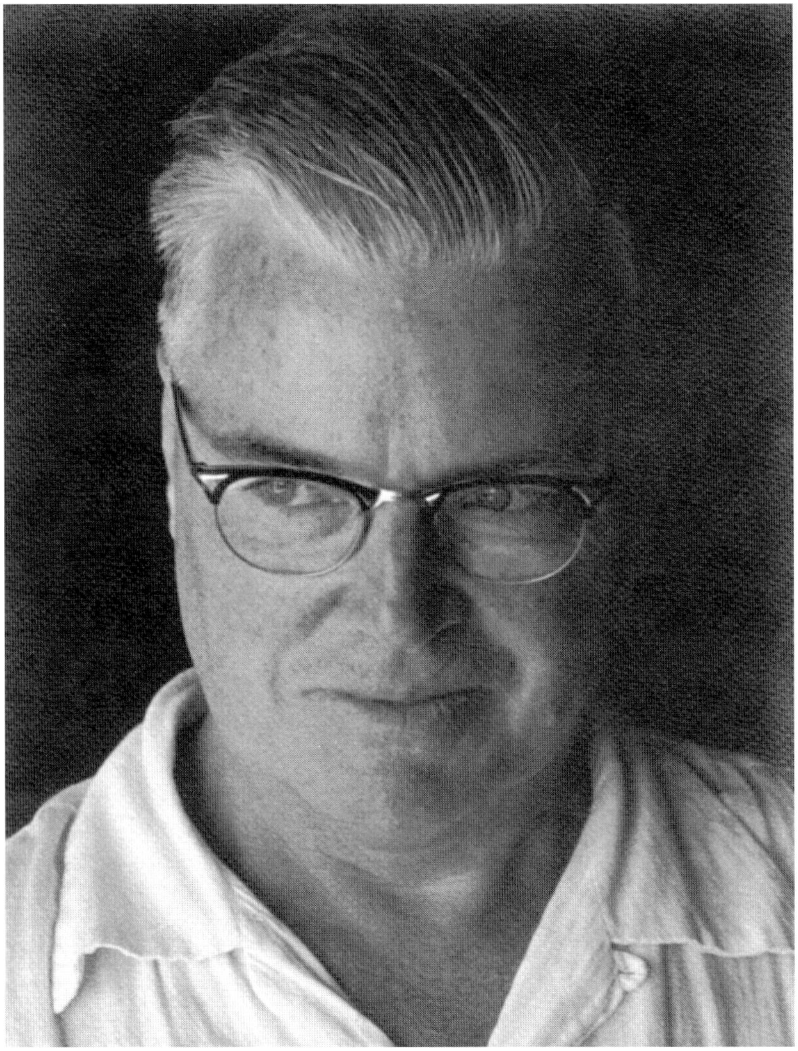

Portrait of Father J. Stanley Murphy, founder of the Christian Culture Series, University of Windsor in Ontario, Canada, taken in 1966.

readers had agreed with Griffin that Rowan was an Uncle Tom. White readers, however, congratulated Rowan on his commonsense approach.

That same long entry of November 26 also contains the discussion of one serious negative aspect of exile – its effect upon Griffin's parents. "I have, of course, realized that they have suffered because of my recent articles and upcoming book on the race issue – suffered from the snubs of the racists and the telephone threats and most of all from fears for my safety. I realized what my conscience had cost them, what loneliness it has brought them at a time in their lives when they need the respect, the affection of people. I have not only exiled myself, I have exiled them, too."

This painful passage gives way immediately to its antidote, both in tone and purpose. He returns to the realm of creative work. "I went to rewash the photographs, great 11x14 prints of my mother to match those I made of Dad – a copy for each of the children." The prints are not merely images of his parents, but lovely artifacts of photographic portraiture.

"Every photo I make, every careful print, and every line I write," he says in that entry, "must soften the heart of someone for the time he witnesses it, must soften in its little way, even for only a few seconds, the great callous that lies on the hearts of so many."

Before the household awoke the next morning, Griffin slept alone in the studio. He woke the following afternoon, and after many cups of coffee, visited the guest house to check on his parents. "Dad appears to be better," he writes in his *Journal.* "He is baking pumpkin pies, always a cheering experience with cheering smells." That was enough to cheer Griffin on and back to work, for he wrote nothing more about it.

That evening supper was shared with his parents and the Berbérs. Luis Berbér tried to convince everyone that they should attend a concert that night to be given by marimba virtuoso, Vida Chenowith; Luis had heard her concert the previous night, performing classical masterpieces. The marimba "sounded unappetizing" to Griffin, but since he admired Berbér's musicology, he went, preparing to be disappointed.

Later that night, November 27, Griffin typed a review of the performance in his *Journal.* Chenowith had opened the program with a Bach Choral and "instantly we knew we were not listening to the marimba of Latin American fiestas, but to an exquisite Baroque organ. She drew from the marimba the

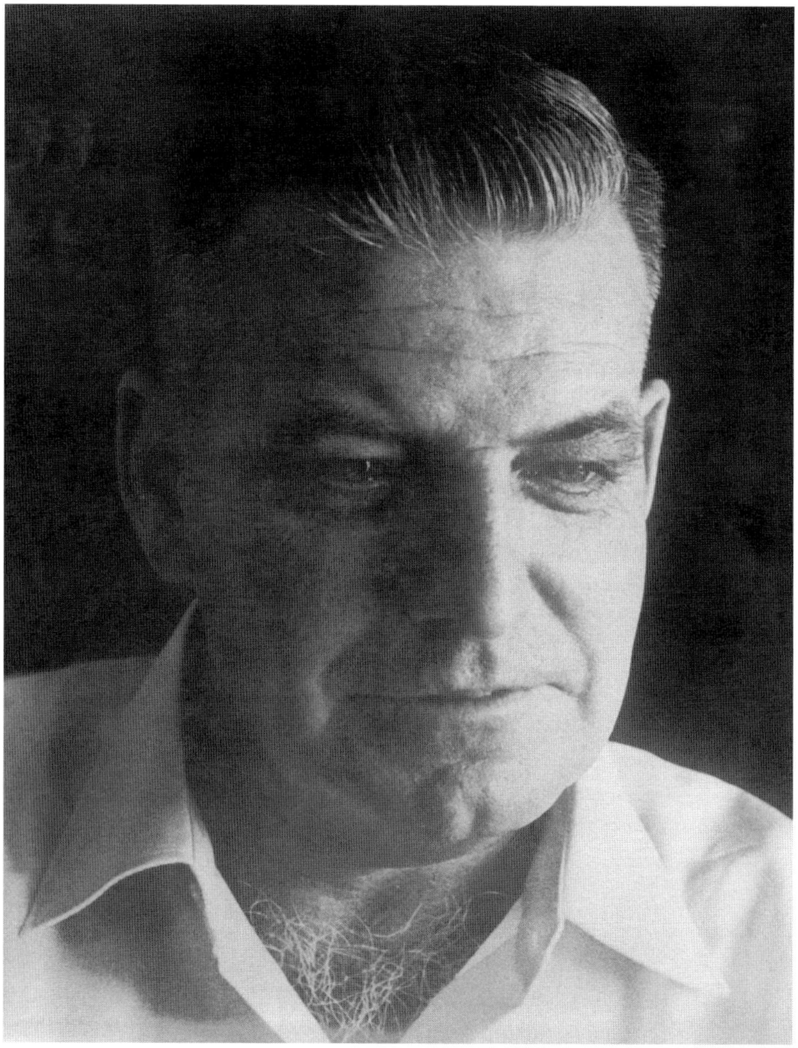

Portrait of Edgar Griffin, older brother of the author, who owned the hacienda in Santa María, where the Griffin family lived after overseeing its renovation.

most incredible (and pure) mixtures of sound. It was Bach of the highest, soberest, and most searching beauty . . . I felt that marvelous thing – the almost unbearable excitement of a first-rate artist doing something new."

The performance continued at the highest level and his review continued with unrestrained enthusiasm, as had the response of the audience, giving the artist standing ovations. But there was just one glitch in the evening:

> The one really revolting fly in the ointment consisted of two American women, who absolutely exhaled arrogance from their expressions, and who looked bored and chewed gum the entire time. I was furious and embarrassed. The other Americans there behaved with perfect decorum, but these two were enough to spoil all Americans in the eyes of the naturally courteous, well-mannered and knowledgeable Mexicans there. They revealed themselves in a way that would have embarrassed them had they cared for the opinions of "those Mexicans." During the Bach, when anyone with a flicker of sensitivity was spellbound, they gum-chewed and gazed about until they obviously saw the only thing that could interest them, the figure of a nude Indian in a giant mural. While Bach's counterpoint sang gloriously, they discerned the fact that a male Indian's buttocks are just about the same as anyone else's.

He was not embarrassed that they were gazing at a giant buttocks, but because they were oblivious to the sublime artistry of Vida Chenowith and J.S. Bach, as well as the apparent cultural decorum of the audience. This joyful musicological (and bawdy sociological) review stirs a postscript about self-scrutiny, unrelated to the music.

> Odd, when people tell me, as one did today, that an article I have written has "such a tone of sincerity about it," I begin to torment myself, certain that I am insincere. Or if they say, "it has in it the ring of truth," I know I must have written it more falsely than I realized. Obvious sincerity in literature is almost the greatest guarantee that one's art has overwhelmed one's true sincerity – great though that may be at the time of writing. What is less sincere

than using techniques to put across a tone of sincerity (again even though one's full sincerity is in it)?

Griffin tended not to be self-conscious while writing, but extremely self-conscious about what he published. When he wondered if a work were good enough, he was asking if he had been "true to the experience or the vision of the work." On the other hand, once he did publish a work he never looked back over his shoulder to admire it.

This had been true for his novels (*The Devil Rides Outside* in 1952 and *Nuni* in 1956) and for non-fiction books apart from those on racism. However, after the publication of *Black Like Me* in the fall of 1961, everything he said or wrote about racism came under the deepest self-scrutiny – since he knew many whites would deny or disagree, and because Griffin never avoided the deeper implications concerning the nature of prejudice. His ethical and moral views demanded that he encounter, understand and strive to transcend his own racism. Thus, the passage about "sincerity" clearly illustrates this self-scrutiny before the first publication of his most famous book.

These questions were at the root of his solitary struggle, but since he would become a "public figure" – indeed, a controversial public figure once he returned to the States – these intimate queries about sincerity and privacy of conscience would become part of the political debate on racism in America (not only in the Deep South). He would succeed so well, and with seeming effortlessness, in the public arena because he kept his focus and everyone's attention on the central issues. Since he never failed at being his own harshest critic, virtually every question asked had been asked over and over in the privacy of conscience. If he thought he had found a solution to the problem, he expressed it; if he was uncertain or did not know the answer, he said so.

As to whether he was sincere or if his work had the "ring of truth": Yes, his sincerity and humility were genuine but, by his own account, he was grossly imperfect. In fact, he was a sinner and knew it; he could fall into the egocentrism of anger or despair, he could bitch and moan in self-pity – in short, he was all too human. But without this deep sense of justice for humanity, his work would have been irrelevant.

During the last week of November 1960, he worked every night in the darkroom. By the beginning of December, he had 200 prints as a result of the marathon, including many 8x10 and 11x14 enlargements. His days were spent overseeing the remodeling of his brother's house. On November 30, the last *Journal* entry until December 29, he noted that the new kitchen had been completed. As the last month of the year was passing, he abandoned the darkroom to revise and expand *Black Like Me*; but as his days grew longer at the construction site, even the writing ceased. By mid-December, he was fully involved in the completion of their new home.

The U-shaped structure, restored from the ruins of a hacienda built 200 years earlier, had taken nearly five months to complete. The large house was a traditional white-washed adobe, its ceiling supported throughout by exposed split-cedar logs, with a red brick floor and a red tile roof. There were three bedrooms and an additional alcove that would be his studio. The living and dining areas were one enormous space, open and naturally lighted. A flagstone courtyard was an open-air garden surrounded by windows and filled with lemon and lime trees and a lush array of flowers. It was furnished by the Shoemakers, who loaned them a houseful of originally-designed wooden pieces. They would eat around a huge refectory table, with matching chairs purchased from the local Benedictine monastery. His studio had a built-in desk and bookshelves. One of the two bath rooms would become the darkroom. The large kitchen, staffed by some of the same villagers who had worked at the Denton House, would become a mecca for indigenous cuisine and the daily baking of bread.

The black metal door at the front of the house opened on to the sidewalk. Across the street was the church and the village water well. There was also a dilapidated structure behind the main house that Griffin hoped to remodel into a larger studio and darkroom (but that project would never be completed). Several days before Christmas, everyone was moving in the direction of their place – family, friends and a crew from the Shoemaker's carried in furniture. By December 23, the family had moved into their "Santa María Hacienda," as Griffin called it. The holiday season had been "glorious" until an accident on December 28 altered the mood and turned all attention upon their youngest child.

> Gregory got kicked in the head by a horse when he tried to pet the animal's hind legs. They brought him in unconscious and so

covered with blood he was unrecognizable. A skull fracture – "an insignificant fracture," according to the doctor as he put in ten stitches – was all the damage, thank God. But do you know that within one minute, every inhabitant of the village was standing at our front door, not making a sound. I was terrified about Gregory, fearing he was dead, but so moved by this demonstration of sympathy I could scarcely bear it. We got him to the hospital and every day while he was there, people anonymously left tortillas, tacos, fruits and cooked dishes at our door. We were fed by the village, never knowing who supplied these things.

By New Years' Eve, four-year-old Gregory had returned home, and everyone was "greatly happy to have him back, though banged up a bit; and the whole house – the weather, the surroundings celebrate." Griffin sat in the courtyard and pronounced it "the most cheerful courtyard in all of Mexico. He played Mozart concerti on the phonograph, listening as the music filled "the air and beyond our walls, the church bells clang while behind us the nuns' hens cackle their delight."

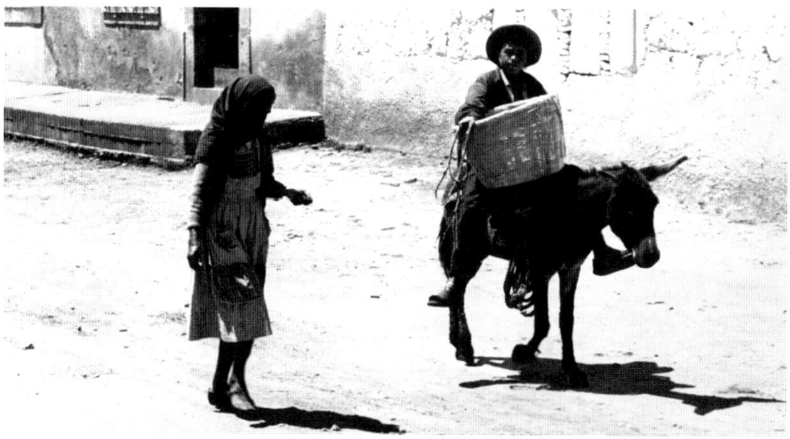

Passions

On January 4, 1961, Griffin had to leave his new-found paradise to fly to New York, where he did two radio shows and a television talk show. On one of the radio appearances, listeners called in their opinions. "Comments ranged everywhere from high praise to denunciation. However, a young historian "gave a really magnificent 'opinion' that would have done Edmund Burke proud, and since he was the last one on the program, he left it on a fine note."

Griffin returned on January 7 and resumed his description of paradise in his *Journal* the following day. "This morning, again in the patio being baked by a mild sun, surrounded by the music of Schumann and the twitterings of thousands of birds in the trees beyond the courtyard wall." At that point, his six-year-old daughter Susan fetched him a tangerine that was "vine-ripe and unbelievably sweet."

> The courtyard is almost too much. It is the first time I've ever tried to work in a place so pleasant I could not settle down to work. Bees hover nearby, along with a hummingbird, sucking at the white blossoms of the lime tree. These blossoms smell of gardenia. The courtyard is completely private, surrounded by a high stone wall that is covered with flowering bougainvillea. Susan has just returned with her doll clothes and sits in a chair nearby. She brings color and enchantment to the courtyard. But I must stop this and get to work.

A few hours later, no work had been done. Elizabeth came in from the market and put a leg of lamb in the oven and a pot of beans on the stove. Then she joined him in the courtyard, deciding to sunbathe. "Now with Mozart going full blast, she drowses in a comfortable chair." Soon he was stripped to the waist and the children, one by one, came to join in the family's sun worship. They relaxed in a what he called a "Riviera" mode, except that all wore large Mexican straw hats.

Since the weather continued to be magnificent, Griffin worked days in the courtyard at the typewriter and continued the darkroom work at night. This early time at the Santa María hacienda proved to be as productive as the period at the Denton House. He wrote Father Stan Murphy on January 19, catching him up on news. The danger for Gregory had passed and the stitches had been removed. Griffin marveled at how the village children treated the American children, how Gregory received special treatment, and that their dialogue was carried on in English, Spanish and Tarascan. It was not only the children, but the entire village that welcomed them as neighbors. Often, when Elizabeth went to Morelia, she took neighbors in the car with her. "There are only two cars he the village," he wrote, "but they never impose for rides – they would not think of it except in an emergency. Such a one occurred the other night when a man knocked at the door and asked if I could take his wife to the hospital." The woman almost gave birth in the back seat, but they made it to Morelia in time.

The only concern in the letter related to Jacques Maritain. "I cannot get Jacques out of my mind. I received the most pitiful letter from him. I wrote him earlier this evening and asked him to come here in the sunshine and recuperate without any worries for as long as he wished." The invitation would not be accepted, for Maritain had other plans being worked out in France.

"The days pass, too busily, and I no longer find the time to write in the *Journal*," he noted on January 27, "and it is a shame, too, because the inclination is constant to put down the life we lead here."

In a January 30 letter to Decherd Turner, he repeated the paradisiacal descriptions of their life in Santa María. He seemed to have only one regret. "How often I wish you lived near enough that I could talk with you. A man has too few friends of your caliber – and idiotically we allow other things to interfere and in the busyness of our days, we lose what is important." Otherwise, he was entirely entranced by the mountain environment.

> This was once the residential section of the aristocrats of Morelia, but a drought drove them out 200 years ago and the place went to ruin. So far, we are the only ones to restore one of the many old houses here. Although we hire as many villagers as possible,

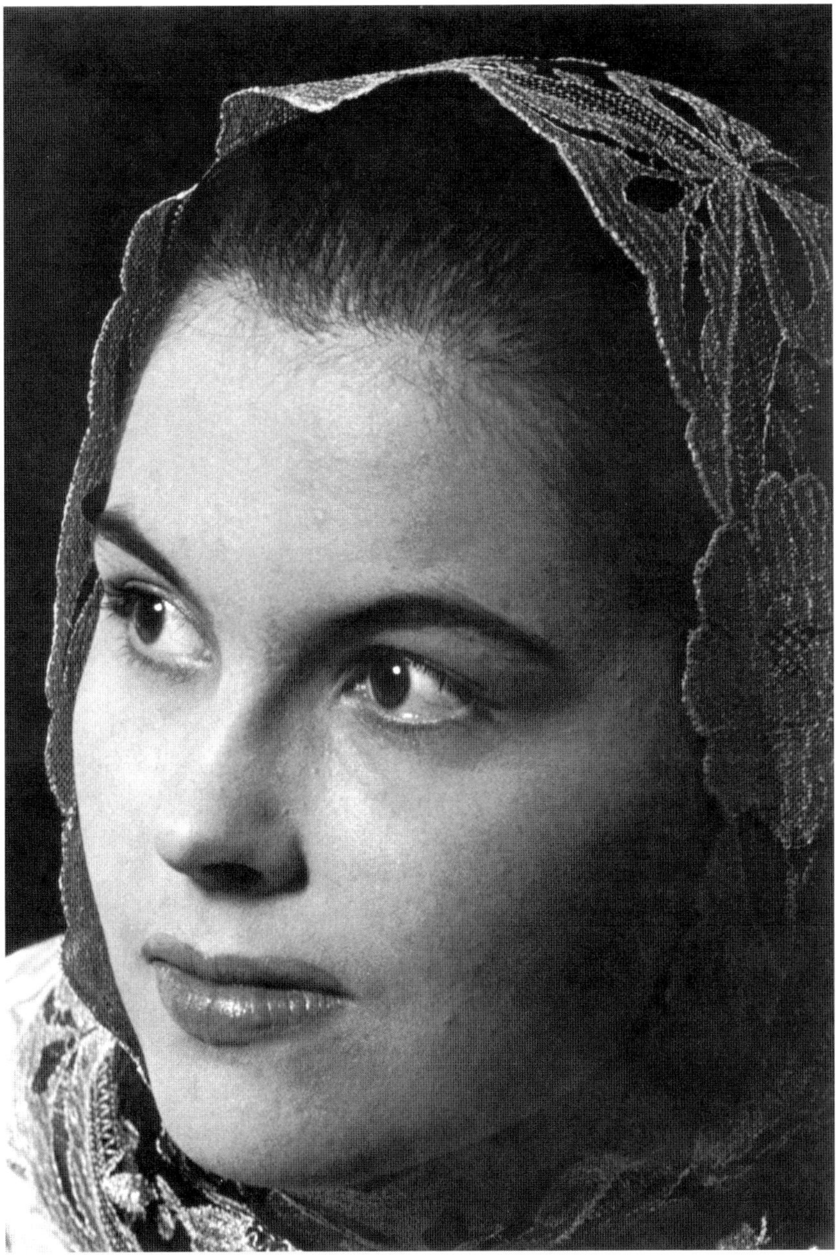

Portrait of Griffin's wife, Elizabeth Ann, taken in 1960 when the family lived in Mexico.

> to give them employment and because help is so embarrassingly cheap here, we have avoided all signorial illusions and are simply neighbors. This is the thing of which I am proudest – I mean that we have succeeded in becoming part of the village rather than remaining in some way separate and above – as so many Americans down here do. I must say that we are absolutely charmed by the place and the people.

On February 1, Griffin made his only *Journal* entry for the month. In the three pages, he reminisced about the early 1940s in France – particularly musical memories about the pianists Gaby and Robert Cassadesus and their children, also gifted musicians. And of Mexico, he remarked that he rarely looked out his windows "without thinking vividly of Graham Greene's *The Power and the Glory*, and how superbly he captured this country."

By mid-February, plans were being made to return to the United States in order to renew their six-month visas. During the last week of that month, the family packed their winter clothes and headed north toward the border. Once back in their cottage west of Mansfield, Griffin began to catch up on stateside business and the family settled in for what was intended to be a brief hiatus.

But during the first week of March, Elizabeth went to bed with a case of the flu. She had *not* been enthusiastic about being in Mansfield, and hoped to return to Mexico as soon as possible. Her total exhaustion reflected the depression that came with being back in a racist atmosphere. Griffin's response to their close proximity to less friendly neighbors was anger. He was also "filled with deep longing to go back to the mountains, to the peace of beauty of the Tarascan Sierras." On March 11, he wrote of that anger about racism and that longing for Mexico in his *Journal*.

> Why? Because in that underdeveloped land there is kindness, courtesy. Why? Because here I am forever made to witness the lowness of men who hate; and because I am not man enough myself to look upon it with sustained pity. No, anger takes me – and the anger is deeper than myself, deeper than anything to do with me, deeper than self-defense. It is the anger of what men

> do to what I symbolize. It is anger at the way things are; at the way men can look and not see what goes on. It is anger – or more exactly black melancholy – that lingers on in me, while the rest of the race shouts its confidence and joy over a better future.

His "black melancholy" was that of "a man who loves his country and is bitterly deceived by the silence of decency and the loudness of indecency." His only relief from it was to be with his family or "to recreate the faces of humanity, the kind faces, the beautiful faces – my photos go entirely in that direction." Writing gave no solace. "My typewriter is silenced, because what I have to say now is neither loving nor beautiful – it is not art, but documentary; and I have not the courage to pour out great efforts for the documentation of men's stupidity." His single entry for that month – and the only one made during those weeks in Mansfield – closed not with his words, but with quotations from Richard Wright and Paul Laurence Dunbar.

On April 2, 1961, Griffin departed alone by car for Mexico, arriving in Santa María on the night of April 4. In the land of the Tarascans, his attention was refocused on their culture – in this instance, attending the annual passion of Christ in Tzintzuntzan.

Tzintzuntzan, in Purépecha, means "place of the hummingbirds." As the ancient capitol city of the Tarascan empire Tzintzuntzan had, at its zenith, been a metropolis of 100,000. When Griffin reached the famous city, he found a small, quiet village. However, for the Tarascans, it remained a sacred place, both in terms of their mythology and in the Catholicism imported by the Spanish that had been so deeply grafted to the original sources.

A Purépecha legend has it that a flock of swallows sought refuge among the tribe when a hawk pursued them. When the hawk swooped down, a warrior killed it with an arrow. Once the hawk struck the ground, the swallows ascended and flew off in separate flocks. It was said that the destiny of the flock was also that of the tribe. The Purépehca then split into four smaller tribes, one remaining in Tzintzuntzan and three others traveling to their eventual places of settlement. "Let us follow the path marked by the flight of swallows," it was said, "and where we find them singing we shall work and live happily." They found the swallows singing in places that became Tingambata, Zacaput, Carapan and Tzintzuntzan.

Interior of the 16th century Franciscan "Monastery of Solitude," located in Tzintzuntzan, the ancient capital of the Tarascan empire.

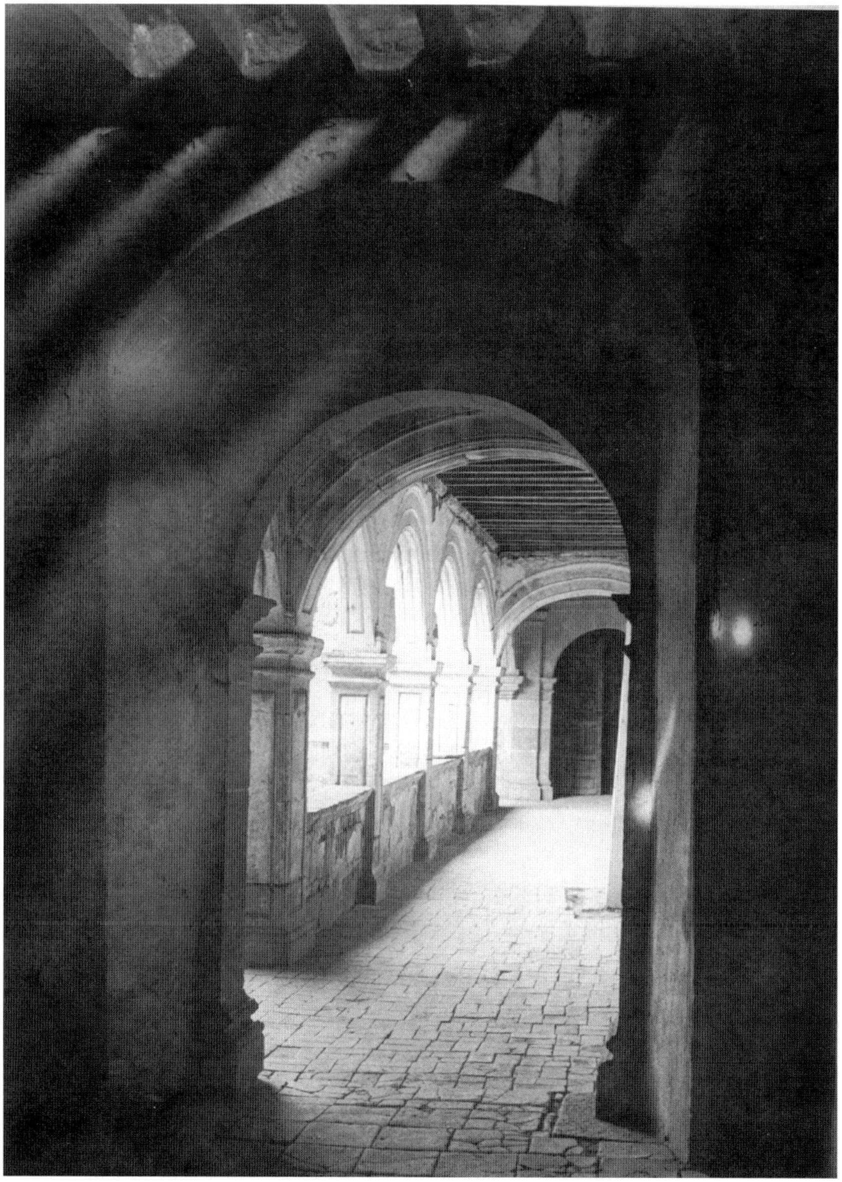

Griffin arrived on Holy Thursday, April 6. He met the last monastic resident at the 16th century Franciscan Monastery of Solitude, Padre Ernesto Tovar, who gave him some background information about the annual ritual. Griffin learned that the role of Christ in the pageant was voluntary. Each year a young man offered to suffer the ordeal, which included all of the physical agonies, except the actual crucifixion. At that point, the young man representing Christ gets taken for medical treatment while a wooden *Cristo* with movable arms and legs gets nailed to the cross. Nearly half of the volunteer Christs die from their ordeal, he was told. When the priest had finished speaking, Griffin asked to look around the monastery. Padre Tovar told him that he should feel at home and, indeed, he had always felt at home in monasteries. He wandered through the second floor corridors and cells, his steps turning up low plumes of dust. He described the scene in "Passion at Tzintzuntzan," a piece that begins tranquilly.

> Odors of stone and age surrounded me. Ghosts of the past hovered over the ruin, telling me that this was once a center of Franciscan learning where friars copied manuscript books on mathematics, philosophy and theology; where they painted frescoes on the courtyard wall depicting the Sacraments.
>
> Drawn to these ghosts, I felt glaringly out of place and time as I opened my case of splendid cameras with their precision optics, set up tripod, and photographed the peeling frescoes.
>
> It was soon done, but I could not leave. I turned at the stairway and walked back down one of the corridors to the last cell on the end. I seated myself on a stone niche carved as a kind of chair against the wall and looked out the hole that had once been a window. Mountain peaks rose in the background. In the foreground below, children played beneath tall jacarandas that were covered with blue blossoms. I sensed some strangeness. Something was not natural in the sights and sounds. It came clear. The children made no sound. Nothing made any sound. Birds were hushed. Except for breeze-stirred leaves, silence brooded over the land. Christ was away, beyond sight and sound, on the Mount of Olives.

Below the window, guards in white "with faceless blood-red hoods" rode on horseback – in search of Christ. The muffled hoof steps, "like the sounds of heartbeats, deepened silence rather than broke it." In the distance he heard an occasional sound that became a musical motif to the silence – "an oboe-like Tarascan shepherd horn sounded its plaintive call, flooding the sunlit countryside with melancholy."

This was not the "black melancholy" he had felt in Texas. However, it was tinged with terror, "despite the brilliant light, the profusion of flowers, and the crowds of Tarascans who streamed toward the compound from neighboring villages."

"The genius of the terror," he speculated, "sprang from the silence, the strange shepherd call in the distance, the growing awareness that Christ, invisible to us, was being searched down." He came down from the second floor and sat on the terrace to reload his cameras – a new Leica and a vintage Alpa.

He spotted the characters of Barabbas and Judas across the compound. Both were wearing "ghastly pink masks" and chasing the children into the church terrace. Suddenly, he was surrounded by the children as the two "villains" moved toward them. Barabbas rattled his chains and asked silently for money. Griffin looked at the children and, receiving no hint of what should be done, looked back at Barabbas, who pushed him to the ground and tried to force him to drink tequila. After a struggle, Griffin pushed him away and reached for his wallet, handing a peso to Barabbas. Judas quickly snatched a five-peso note and then both thieves skipped away.

The children's reproaches made clear that he made a poor decision. He had contributed his part of the thirty pieces of silver. He wanted to exonerate himself in the eyes of the children, so he rushed after the thieves. Eventually, he coaxed the thieves into putting the pesos into the church's alms box. He had corrected his error and the children no longer feared the American with the camera equipment.

Despite the fact that he knew these were actors, Griffin began to feel the hypnotic effect of the ritual. "We were so involved that I found it difficult to realize that this was essentially an *ad libitum* play. I felt split, part realizing this was the 20th century, part eerily involved in the event 2000 years ago." This sense of being split hereafter accounts for the different tones and varied pacing of the essay, as alternately, Griffin becomes an observing camera-eye and a participant in the ritual – and in both modes, his attempt at conscious planning gets swiftly reduced to reflexive action.

Later that afternoon the Tarascan Christ was being pushed by the guards into the compound. The kiss of Judas had already occurred off stage, and now the Passion was escalating in cruelty. An American woman and her young son were in the crowd. Seeing the blood streaming down the face of Christ, she said, "That's enough for me," and dragged away the boy. "I think it was not the cruelty of the scene so much," Griffin speculated, "as the incredible illusion that this man was Christ, that we participated in the Passion, that it went far beyond the niceties of play-acting."

This Passion was no polite aesthetic catharsis and no Biblical morality play. Even in Griffin's black and white photographs, as well as the color slides he took with the Alpa, there is a certain unreality in the images. The slides capture a textured palette of garish colors and antic forms, but they are not particularly distinguished. The action scenes do not "breathe" in the color slides. His true mastery was in the subtle gradations of the black and white prints. There is a perfect print of the wooden *Cristo* and contemplative images of the monastery, reminding one of frames from early films by Ingmar Bergmann.

After a perfunctory trial and condemnation, the Tarascan Christ was dragged from the compound and locked away in a cell, where he would not receive food or water or medical attention during the night. Some of the crowd remained to pray, but most departed. It was then that the shepherd horn was heard again, sending out "its desolate call through the moonlit night," like a coda to Holy Thursday. By midnight, Griffin located a place of lodging; exhausted, he slept through the cold night.

On April 7, Good Friday morning, he was served a generous breakfast "in a beautiful old kitchen that opened out on a courtyard crowded with flowers and children." He watched barefooted Tarascan girls walk past, wondering how it might have been when this village of 500 had been the capitol of the empire.

He walked to the church where a group of men carried the wooden *Cristo* outside to a pair of saw-horses in the courtyard, and began cleaning it. "A large, elderly, tough-looking matriarch sent them away and took over the work. When she bent over to kiss the body, I prepared to photograph. She commanded me not to make photographs."

He explained that he had received Padre Tovar's permission. She snorted in disgust and demanded money. He asked why, since Christ belonged to everyone. She was amused by the indirect insult, but would not budge. "I certainly don't intend to pay for every shot as I take it. And when I do pay, I'll give it to the priest, not some old woman." Griffin played out the game of insults when she continued to refuse permission without being paid. "All you want from your relationship with Christ is money," he declared and asked her to step away so he could photograph the *Cristo*. Appreciating the quality of his insults, she finally agreed.

"Now you are being amiable," he laughed. He went over to the statue and asked that she kiss the *Cristo*. Coyly, she asked, "How?" He leaned over to demonstrate.

> My lips almost touched the statue's cheek when her doubled fist smashed hard against my temple, knocking me back against the wall. The blow stunned me. She folded her arms and stood majestic, her smile suppressed behind wrinkled lips.
>
> "Who do you think you are?" I shouted, struggling against my humiliation and rage. "You think you own Christ . . . ." I advanced toward her. She shook her finger slowly from side to side and stared me down.
>
> "Only Judas kisses Christ's cheek in this season."
>
> I looked at her dumbfounded as it came to me that she had saved me from being Judas. Gratitude replaced my anger.
>
> "Kiss the body, but not the cheek," she said.
>
> Her triumph was total but not unkind. She could afford to be magnanimous now that she had shown that a simple Tarascan hill peasant carried the Gospels in her very veins and heart and instincts as part of even her most spontaneous reactions, whereas the gringo outsider carried them only in his head and could forget them.

Griffin left for the compound where the crowd had gathered. Near the cell of the imprisoned Christ, he encountered two guards who raised their

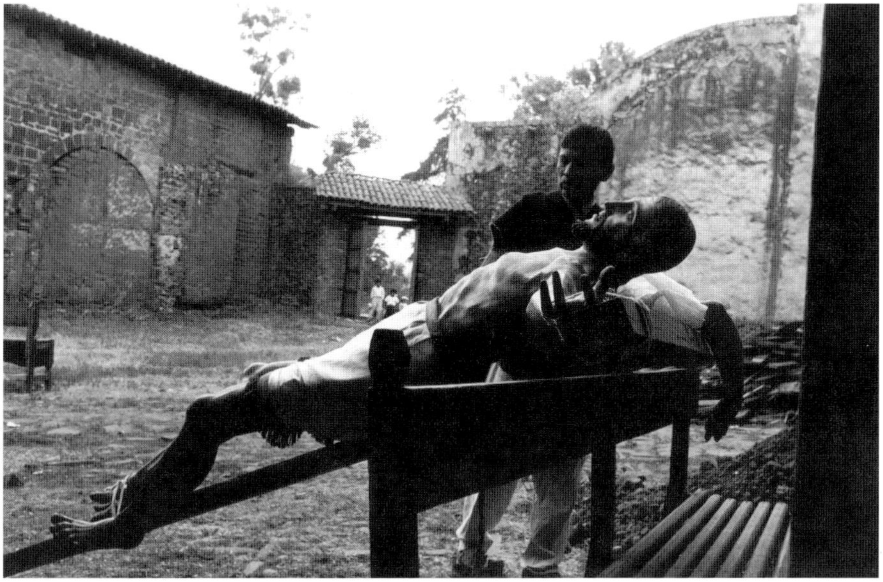

A Tarascan man readies the wooden *Cristo* used in the Passion of Christ, the annual event which takes place in Tzintzuntzan.

spears as he raised his camera. He tried to explain that he had permission to photograph, but there was no response from behind the red hoods. When he raised the camera again, a spear knocked the lens cap aside; and when he tried a third time, he was struck on the side of the head. Instinctively, he reached for a spear and jerked it so violently that the guard fell to the ground. He tossed the spear aside and photographed the other guard. The crowd voiced their support of his actions. However, he realized that they were living their roles and felt sympathy for the fallen guard. "I was overwhelmed with my own sense of guilt at altering historical truth in this manner. Two thousand years ago no photographer had thus embarrassed Christ's guards. My action distorted the truth of the day, changed it from what it should have been."

Suddenly, the crowd's attention was drawn to a loud voice that ordered the Christ be brought forth. It was a centurion on horseback and he approached the cell with four guards. The haggard Christ, streaked with his own dried blood, was dragged from the cell. He was shoved to the other side of the compound where he was stripped and flogged. Without a word, he endured the relentless whipping until his bare back was covered with blood. Next, the scene of Pilate washing his hands was reenacted.

The Christ was then clothed in purple and a heavy wooden cross was loaded onto his shoulders. The young Tarascan was pushed toward Calvary. Griffin moved ahead of the procession to be in a position to photograph Christ's approach, stepping into the dusty path and moving away as he shot film. Barabbas, who was dancing gleefully ahead of the dragging cross, swung heavy chains against the photographer's legs, knocking him off-balance. "I concentrated away from the drubbing and photographed the Christ, his face hazed with pain in strange repose. I photographed the crowd of men and women, their eyes forlorn with tenderness and grief. Again, I burned with the embarrassment of my intrusion. Cameras did not belong in the Passion."

Just then, the Christ fell forward in the red dust. Again forgetting himself, Griffin hurried to help lift up the Christ, but felt a spear jabbing his torso. "Intense silence surrounded all of this activity" and, in the distance, the shepherd horn could be heard, "accompanied by savage thuds as the guards beat Christ until he staggered to his feet." Griffin knelt in the path to get a close-up while Barabbas' chains pounded his back. He lost balance and fell forward as the Christ approached.

> His eyes were dazed. I froze, fearing he would stumble over me. I rolled on my back and reversed position, trying to scoot out of his way. As his foot touched mine, he stopped. His glassy eyes cleared. He looked down on me patiently, intelligently, and with an expression of such sorrowful love that I felt devastated. I reminded myself that this was not Christ, but a Tarascan youth playing the role. It did no good. The illusion was too powerful.

Griffin had been transfixed for that instant in the presence of Christ, even though he "brutally reminded" himself that this was *not the real Christ.* He was stunned by this powerful illusion which brought him face to face with a transcendent expression radiating pure compassion. Griffin writes of a confusion of realms: the historical Passion of Christ, the Tarascan ritual of reenactment and his own complex passions. Swept up in mystery, he is a penitent drawn inexorably along the path of human tragedy and the outsider who intrudes upon the sacred procession with a camera.

The stark contrast between this piece about the Passion and "The Watch of the Dead" cannot be exaggerated. At the Watch, he attempts to disappear into the darkness, careful not to intrude upon the dignified rhythms of the native ritual. Yet at the Passion, he cannot control himself, blundering at crucial times. During that instant of encountering the Christ, he "realized that my instincts as a photographer were functioning, that I was working the camera, photographing first his face and then his blood-stained feet." He was driven not merely to witness the Passion but to "capture" it on film. As Christ passed, "the frightful stench . . . filled my nostrils, odors of sweat and souring blood . . . the total degradation of the God-Man" brought him to an awareness of having been caught up in "a weird implacable madness." After that, he continued photographing, but from a respectful distance.

As he filmed the "almost nonchalant cruelty" of the stumbling Christ, a piglet crossed in front of the cross; a moment later, a hen pecked the dried blood on the Tarascan's feet. Then, the ridiculous gave way to the sublime.

> At the point where tensions could no longer be borne, an exquisite, white-clad Tarascan girl, representing the Virgin, detached from the crowd and ran in a great floating motion toward Christ.
>
> His eyes again cleared. He knelt on one knee and received her into his arms. She embraced the blood and stench. All action stopped. The madness vanished from the crowd. The gesture was so filled with tenderness that even Christ's eyes filled with tears that diluted the blood on his cheeks. . . . Anger was defeated in us.

Christ's walk to Calvary continued until the young Tarascan reached the church and was carried through a curtained doorway. He was replaced by the wooden *Cristo*, which was nailed to the cross. Then an elderly man went into the sanctuary and knelt at the foot of the cross. He "stared up at the figure and, with his arms outstretched in a gesture of abandon, began to intone a Tarascan chant, slow and flowing as an ocean wave." The crowd went to its knees and joined in the dirge, which "resounded through the countryside."

Griffin left the church through a side door and walked across the empty compound. On the way to the village, he encountered a messenger who announced that the young Tarascan Christ would live.

Beyond the chanting, he heard the last mournful sounding of the shepherd's horn.

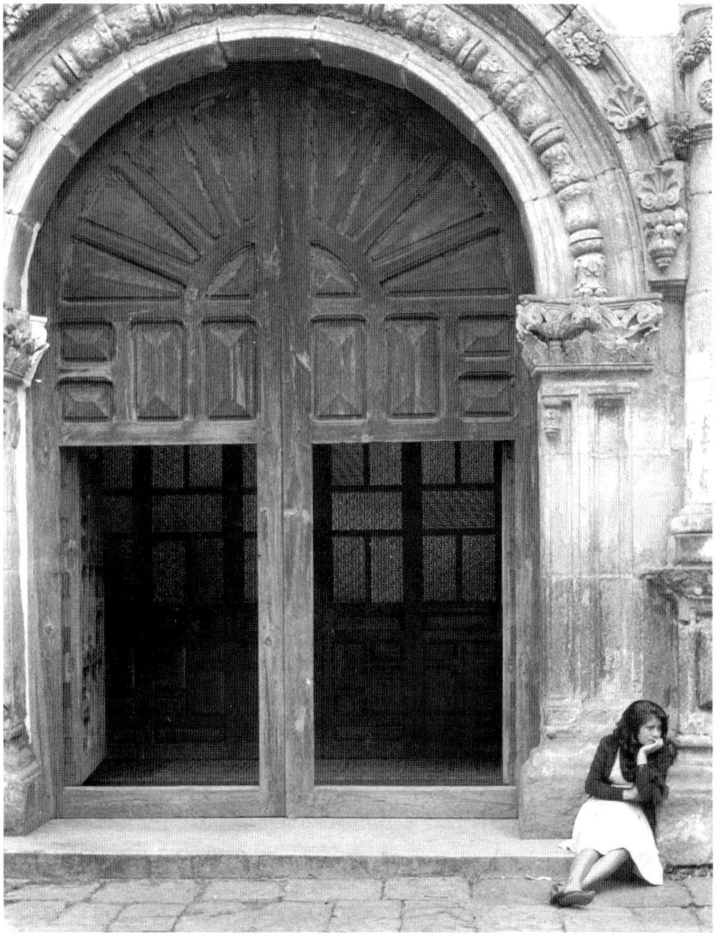

Dissonance

During the next week, Griffin immersed his energies in darkroom work, excited by the images that were emerging from twenty rolls of film, and also because he missed the company of Elizabeth and their three children.

On April 15, Sallie and Hannah Gillespie arrived from Taos for a visit. "How good it is to have them here," Griffin wrote in the *Journal* on April 16, "not only to see them again, as dear and old friends, but to dissipate the almost unbearable loneliness of the place since the family is not here. Without them I begin to be paralyzed by the consuming depression of not hearing their voices, seeing them, holding them."

On April 17, he took the Gillespie sisters to hear *Los Niños Cantores* perform under the baton of Luis Bebér in Morelia. "It undid us all," he writes in the *Journal,* to hear them sing the works of Palestrina, Pergolesi, Orff and Stravinsky. "They sang spectacularly – flawless counterpoint, difficult dissonant counterpoint, with such a flair and precision and attack and tonal parity that it tied us up in knots and left us exhausted."

What he heard later that evening on the radio would become the ultimate dissonance to his brief paradisical life at the Santa María hacienda. There were various reports from Russian, Cuban and North American sources concerning what would later become known as the disastrous Bay of Pigs invasion of Cuba – propaganda from the communists and denials from the States. The effect of this event would impact on Americans living in Mexico, especially those living in and near Morelia.

The next afternoon, Luis Berbér brought bad news. An organized group of university students had invaded the Mexican-North American Cultural Institute in Morelia that morning. "They broke into the Institute," Luis said, and "hauled everything into the street and set a great bonfire." Griffin pleaded with him to be cautious and not be seen with Americans. The Tarascan conductor would not hear these pleas, but insisted that Griffin move his manuscripts, paintings and darkroom equipment to Luis' home, since American houses would be targeted.

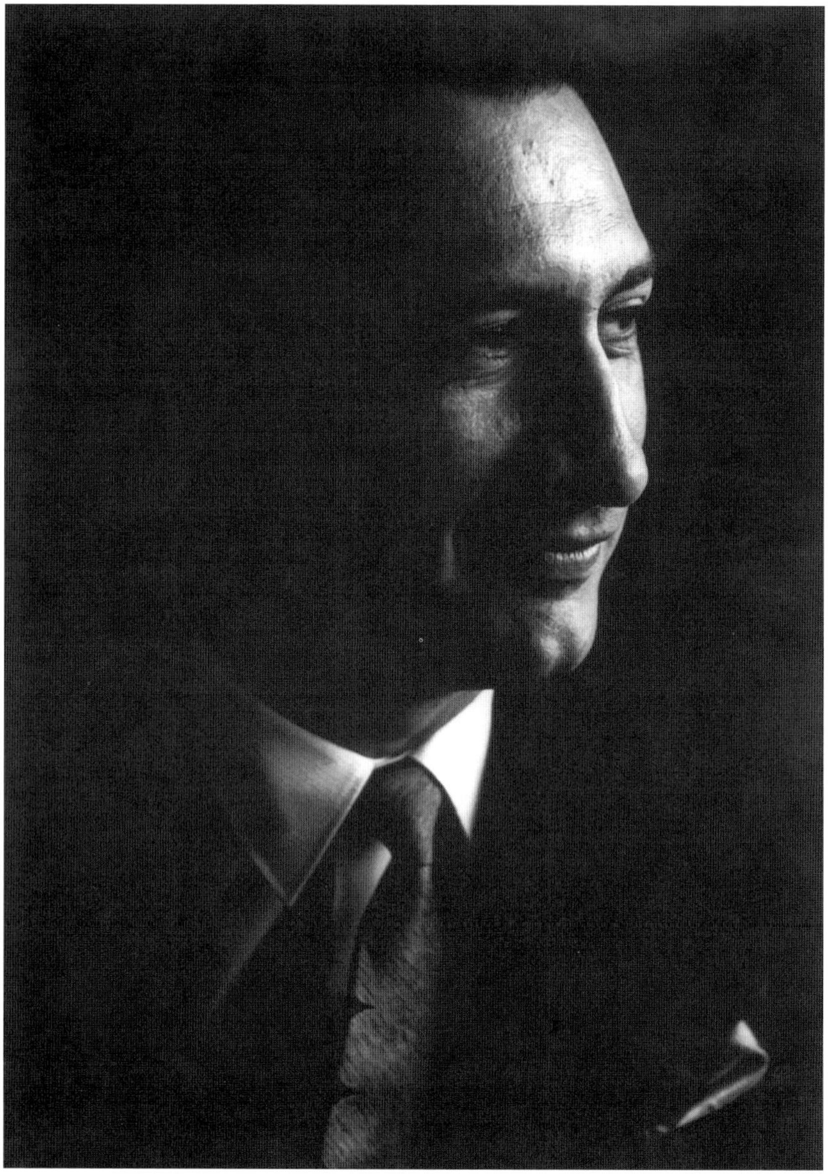

Tarascan Luis Berbér, the conductor and director of the world-famous boys' choir, *Niños Cantores de Morelia*. Griffin met Berbér in 1960, and they became life-long friends. This 1964 portrait appeared in *The John Howard Griffin Reader* (1968).

Griffin's *Journal* entry of April 18 runs 15 pages.

> We pieced together the sequence of events. As planned, the students met ostensibly to protest U.S. intervention in Cuba. Faculty members of the University of St. Nicholas harangued the students into a ferment against U.S. citizens. At 11:30, the governor's secretary met with the communist student leaders. Director Eugene Kenny, his wife, and two American friends were in the Institute. Two policemen arrived to protect them.

But when the demonstrators marched there, they smashed through the doors and vandalized the Institute. The police did nothing, but the Americans escaped unharmed.

Griffin was on the phone calling Americans to brief them on the danger and to invite all to a strategy meeting inside the formidable walls of the Denton Estate. At five, Luis returned from Morelia. "Get your parents quickly," he said. "The mob is coming to burn the hill."

"Where are we going?" Griffin asked.

"To my house – they won't think to look for anyone there."

"What about the other Americans?"

"They've been warned. They'll all go to the hotel or the seminary, but I want you and your parents at my place – hurry."

He told Luis that he had to stick with the others. "To the best of my knowledge," he writes in his *Journal,* "I was the only person there with experience in crisis-community techniques. In an emergency I would be needed. Too, I did not want our presence in his home to cost him reprisals." As a student in France, Griffin had been trained as a medic; as a volunteer in the French Underground he had assisted Jewish families in escaping the Nazis. After being run out of France by the Gestapo, he joined the Air Force and served for three years in the South Pacific, where he was wounded.

Griffin drove the Gillespies and his parents to the mountainside hotel that night. Then he went to the nearby seminary to use the telephone. It was the only telephone in the village besides that of José Tocaven, who lived nearby. Tocaven was the editor of *La Voz de Michoacán,* the state's largest newspaper, which had been propagandizing against American citizens in Morelia. Griffin decided to register a protest with the newspaper editor. "Why should I do anything to help you," Tocaven said, "when at this moment Americans are murdering our Cuban brothers in the streets of Havana?"

"The Santa María Tarascans are our friends," Griffin told the editor. "They will kill any student who comes up this hill. Such deaths will be your responsibility, since you have agitated against us. Also, this will probably so enrage the Tarascans that they'll come here and kill you." The warning got the newspaper editor's attention.

"I guarantee you it is nothing. They will not harm you. It is only an innocent demonstration," Tocavan said. Griffin replied that if the mob arrived, the editor would have to face it on his own.

At the seminary, a young priest telephoned the federal office in Morelia, asking for troops. The request went quickly through the chain of command. An officer called back to say the mob had swelled to several thousand. The young priest hung up and said: "Troops are on their way, but we do not know if they will get here in time. You are in grave danger. Take the women and children at once to the Benedictine monastery on the mountain. If the mob gets this far, we'll see they get no further."

"How can you be sure?" Griffin asked the priest.

"We have three hundred seminarians," the priest said, smiling. "All are in superb physical condition. They will block the road."

Griffin went to his car, where he saw some of the seminarians at the gate. They were in their best cassocks, smiling, looking eager for the clash. He returned to the hotel to gather the Americans for the drive to the monastery.

On the return trip, they encountered the young priest. He spoke to Griffin in French, not wanting to frighten the other Americans. "The troops are at the bottom of the hill. The crowd will be intercepted." The mob was only five minutes away from a possible clash with the troops. The priest wanted to know if the Shoemakers were back from America.

"No, Father. But I warned the men to lock up and stay there all night."

"Good. It seems the crowd has instructions to burn them out."

"Why?" Griffin asked.

"They are important people in the village. Ruining them would put many out of work and make it easier for the communists."

With his parents and the Gillespie sisters, Griffin led a caravan in four automobiles up the mountain to the monastery. The Americans were welcomed by the monks and given soft drinks. He comments in his *Journal* that the faces of the Americans "were calm in the dim light, but drawn with strain. Most were middle-aged, had never been subjected to this sort of crisis, and were bewildered to find themselves fugitives from a mob's anger."

Griffin returned to the village, where federal soldiers patrolled the streets and Tarascan villagers had organized. When he drove to check on the Shoemaker's house and shop, he saw Tarascan men on the roof. "The men are on watch," the foreman told him, "and the women have set up a shrine to Our Lady of Guadalupe, and will burn candles and pray all night." At the seminary he learned from the priest that the mob had been disbanded and that all was quiet in Morelia. Griffin returned with the news and the Americans decided to stay the night at the hotel. The soldiers returned to Morelia, but the village continued being guarded by police patrol cars.

Back in the hacienda before midnight, Griffin began to make notes about the day's events. After midnight, he decided to drive in widening circles around the village. He saw no patrol cars, but the village was being protected by Tarascan men with rifles and machetes. He droved down into the valley to investigate Morelia during the pre-dawn hours. There he "did not find a single patrol car or policeman. I drove through the silent streets that earlier had been feverish with the mob."

On Morelia's main street, young men were pasting up copies of a poster that read: DEATH TO THE YANKEE ASSASINS OF CUBA, and the store fronts were covered.

> I did every suspicious thing I could think of to draw the attention of the police. I drove slowly, stopped and got out to study the posters (leaving the engine running), and even tore down some posters. Still no one came. Down the street, the young men continued their work. I drove closer to them. With exaggerated gestures I pretended to photograph them as I drove slowly past. These "enemies" turned and waved gallantly. They knew I was American, driving a car with an American license, yet they showed only cordiality. Finally, I stopped the car. We exchanged greetings.

"May I photograph you pasting these posters?" I asked.

They graciously assented and posed while I clicked the empty camera. I asked them why, since they were pasting admonitions to kill all Yankees, they were friendly to me. They laughed and told me it was a job, like any other. I offered them cigarettes.

"In other words, if I paid you to paste up anti-communist posters, you would do it?

"Why not?" they laughed.

On April 19 there was more anti-American propaganda in *La Voz de Michoacán,* as well as praise for the destruction of the Institute. Tarascans from the village dropped by to check on Griffin. "With superb delicacy, avoiding the subject, they manage to convey their apologies for the shameful incidents." They indicated that Tocaven had sold out for a price to the communists and they considered him an enemy.

Griffin went to see his parents. Word came to hide their cars and lock the gate. They heard another demonstration at the bottom of the hill where soldiers were on guard. The Gillespie sisters urged his parents to return with them to Taos until the crisis was over. They refused to go without their son. He convinced them that he would be freer to work and to escape if they were out of harm's way. Many of the Americans in the village had departed for home; those who remained gathered at the hotel for supper.

Newscasts described the riots in Morelia and other riots in Mexico and Latin America. Griffin believed that the "spontaneous" riots were all part of a world-wide outbreak of well-planned communist demonstrations. He also learned that sound trucks had broadcast anti-Catholic slurs along with the anti-American propaganda. "This last move astonishes me, since most here are Catholics, and it would seem a perfect device to alienate them."

The next morning, April 20, his parents began packing. Luis Berbér arrived to let them know he would drive them to the train. He pulled Griffin aside to tell him that he had confronted Tocaven. "As a Mexican, I told him I was ashamed to see another act so. I told him these communist rioters were students, and what did they destroy? Books and recordings and equipment that would teach our people. They destroyed culture. Do you know what he did? He laughed and then said: 'When the Nazis turned against the Jews, the first thing they did was destroy the Jewish archives, destroy their culture.'"

After Luis had driven his parents to the railway station, Griffin writes in his *Journal:*

> My parents are gone. I sit in their house, where I shall sleep the next few nights (since I can hide my car here). The house is full of the debris of their hasty departure, full of echoes. The doors and windows are open to spring night in the Sierras. All around me, in the dark, Tarascan men watch and wait. The horror here has succeeded in accomplishing the communist goals. The local citizens, at least too many of them, are now convinced U.S. troops did all the fighting in Cuba, and that the great U.S. monster is intent on swallowing up Mexico. We have not given answer to any of Tocaven's charges. Our refusal to do so (or our inability to do so) amounts to tacit admission of our guilt.
>
> Tonight the great issues evade me. What I see is that the communists, the cheaters against humanity, drive decent elderly people (and there are many more than my parents) to abandon their homes, their dignity as humans. Tonight the communists hatch their plots, tirelessly, while people leave their homes, filled with tears at the heroism of their Tarascan friends.

On April 21, three members of the U.S. Embassy in Mexico City arrived to look into the anti-American demonstrations, and the governor had troops protect the evening's meeting. Griffin met with the three officials later. "I let them know that this great show of 'control' was new on the part of the local government." They told him that the governor rationalized the Institute burning as simply "a spontaneous student manifestation that got out of hand." Griffin gave them the names of the "Russian instigators" and student leaders paid by the Russian embassy. They asked for a full report, which was delivered by government courier to the U.S. Embassy in Mexico City within a few days. He rerouted all his other mailings through Celaya instead of Morelia, because he was convinced that his mail was being illegally intercepted.

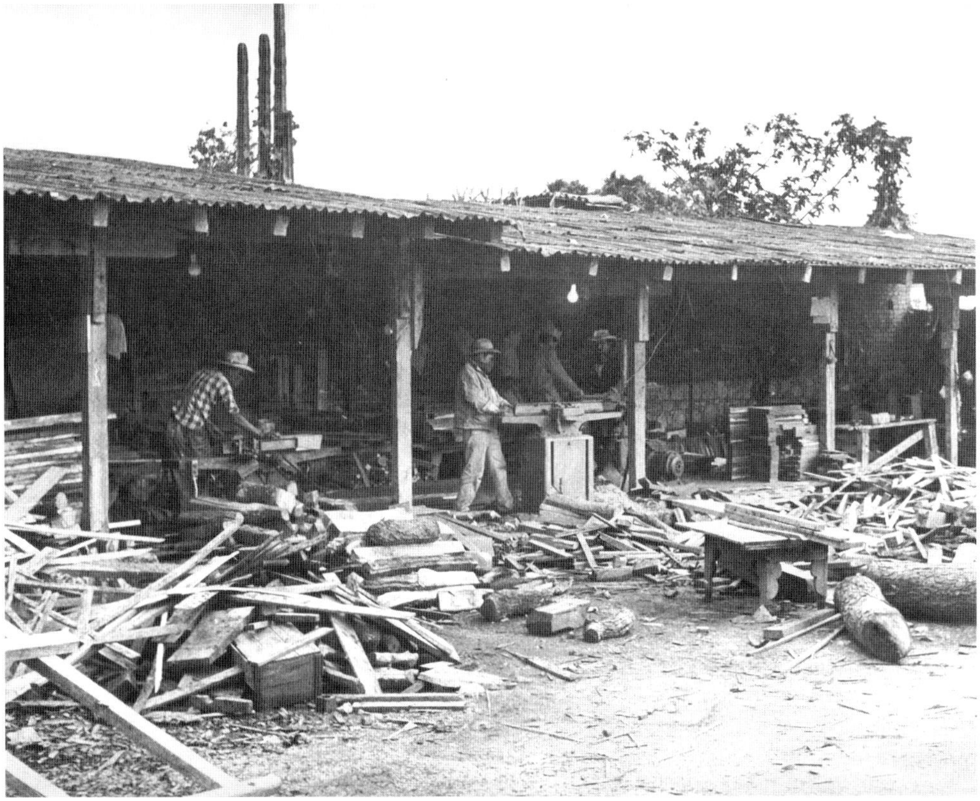

The woodworking shop owned by the Americans Barbara and Don Shoemaker, who lived in the village of Santa María and were friends of the Griffins.

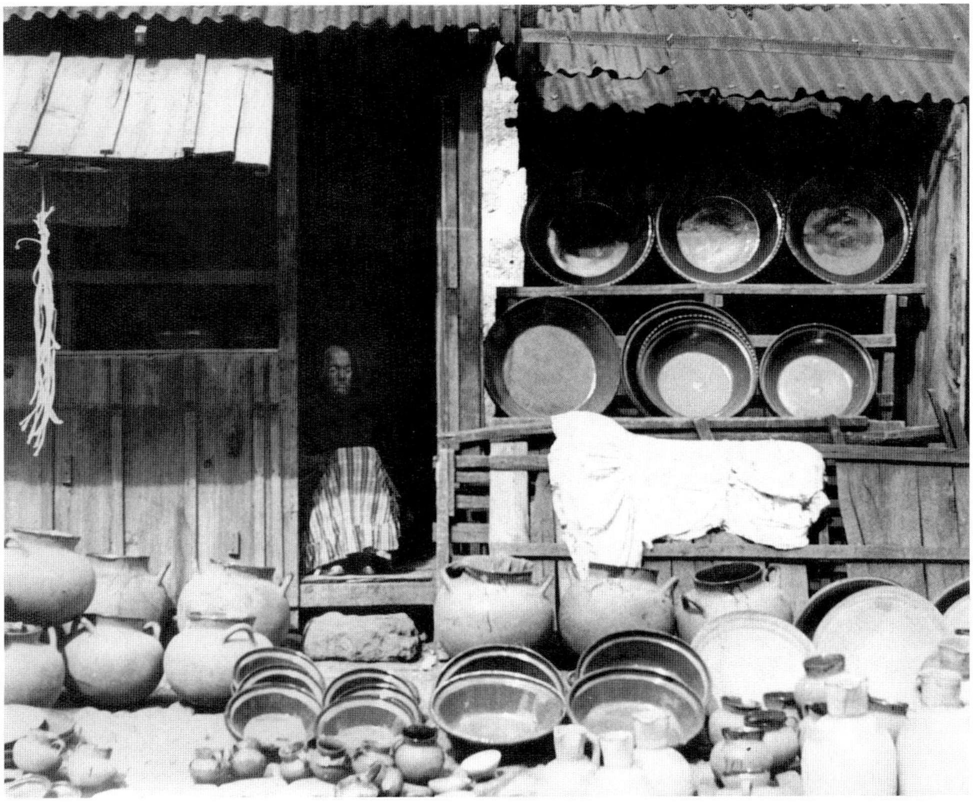

Tarascan woman sitting in the doorway of her shop in the village of Santa María.

On April 23, Griffin read a copy of Mexico City's *Excelsior*, one of nation's finest newspapers. "They give an accurate, objective report. They tell it straight. They name the Russian agents who came here, and they name the student leader. No one in Morelia can now doubt that this was a plot of international communism – that it was treason committed against Mexico. Tocaven had run the photo of the burning Institute, gloatingly, as a symbol of the defeat of 'American Imperialism.' *Excelsior* ran the same photo, and in context with their article, it looked shameful."

During the morning of April 24, he began proofing the galleys of *Black Like Me*, which had been shipped by courier from Houghton Mifflin in Boston. A week later, the galleys were corrected and shipped by courier to Boston. There remained only a few additions and clarifications to make and the book's Preface to compose.

Nonetheless, Griffin was reluctant to leave Santa María. "We had a few peaceful and lovely months here," he notes in his *Journal* (May 2, 1961), "and now I must return to what? – to the hate, the taunts, the threats, the endless busy activity, the stupidity of men who have become expert in destroying reputations (since they cannot destroy arguments). I need to work, but I feel exhausted. I need to see my wife and children, but how I dread to return to that racist-ridden area. . . ."

On May 4, he was packing what his parents had left behind. He found his mother's "family album" – filled with photographs of her children, report cards of all four, newspaper articles from the 1950s, postcards he had sent her from overseas, and all the "things that made her proud."

> It was a poignant glimpse into the heart of a mother. With what care did she paste and date these items. Such things tear me up. It is my pity for these parents, who should have things good, who should have security and peace at their age, that turns me bitter with loathing against the racists and the communists who have driven them out of their last two homes. Yet, it is my doing – I have fought them all – the nazis, the fascists, the racists, the communists . . . but now, in view of what they have done to my parents (and to how many other innocent ones?), I can stir only loathing for them.

The next day, when he checked the post office box in Morelia, it was empty once again. He had not heard from his wife in nearly three weeks and there had been no word from his parents at the Gillespies in Taos. He inquired at the post office, but they knew nothing about any missing mail. He was convinced that his lines of communication had been severed. That afternoon, May 5, he called his wife in Mansfield. Elizabeth confirmed that no mail had arrived there either, even though he had written her nearly every day. She urged him "to get the hell out of there."

That same day's edition of *Excelsior* continued its excellent coverage of the crisis, including an interview with Eugene Kenny, who described the student assault accurately. Most in the village had read the recent issues of *Excelsior,* and he felt that "the tide is turning." He received waves and smiles on car trips between Santa María and Morelia, feeling that the villagers, at least, realized that the political plot had been exposed. Even in Morelia, the people were asking why the Russian agents had not been expelled from Mexico, and suggesting loudly that those who led the riot should be arrested.

Tocaven's newspaper quoted the governor as a headline which read: "WE HAVE NO COMMUNISTS IN MICHOACÁN." Local officials in Morelia were involved in downplaying the incident, claiming that it had all been a mistake; and had they known how the crowd would get out of control, they would have stopped it.

Five days later, on May 10, there was still no mail in his postal box. "By cutting off my mail," he says in his *Journal*, "they have cut off my tongue, forcing me to leave." He had prepared for that eventuality. That evening he had dinner with Kenny and several other Americans in Morelia. "All of us felt that this was a salvageable situation now that Excelsior was giving answers to the lies printed in *La Voz de Michoacán*."

Griffin was preparing that night in order to leave the next morning. "I have never lived among a people for whom I have felt such admiration and love as I do the Tarascans." His family would never return to live in their beloved "Santa María Hacienda."

That final night and into the morning hours Griffin listened to the music of Gabrieli on the radio, which "turned the night magical." The valley below and the village gardens were basked in the ivory light of a full moon. He listened to a lone cricket, realizing that it was "the end for me here."

He thought of the Tarascans asleep in the village, "with their trust in Nature and God and Humanity, their absolute fidelity and generosity."

He viewed the political picture as being "virtually complete," and the recent events as having been prototypical of totalitarian group techniques in crisis communities worldwide. "It would have succeeded completely, except for the splendid cooperation of the North Americans and Mexicans, plus *Excelsior's* gallant coverage. Now, on the contrary, the counter emotion has taken hold. They clearly see that acts which passed under the guise of 'patriotism' were in reality treason. I think this area will be won back to a clear concept of where their future lies – with Mexico rather than Russia."

A little after daybreak, he packed everything into the car. He knew that a long and lonely trip lay ahead, as he left the village heading north toward Texas.

Black Like Me

By the middle of May, 1961, Griffin was being hounded by reporters about his return to Mansfield. Various reports from "reliable sources" suggested that he had been driven out of Mexico. One local headline, from the *Fort Worth Star-Telegram,* blared the question: AUTHOR DRIVEN OUT OF MEXICO BY REDS? The article included a photo of the author, and began: "John Howard Griffin, the blind Mansfield author who regained his sight, said today that he left Mexico because of 'pressure' from communists there who objected to the articles he wrote. The 40-year-old novelist appeared reluctant to talk about his reasons for leaving Mexico." He was indeed reluctant to discuss the situation because the turmoil in Morelia had remained unresolved. Also, concern about local reprisals against his family had become paramount once again. When asked about his intention to stay in Mansfield: "You might say we're visiting here," was the way he phrased it, without masking his sarcasm. He felt only revulsion for Mansfield. His deepest hope had been to return to Mexico, but even with a complete resolution of the tense political climate in Morelia, he could not have returned then, since he was flat broke. It was not the first time, and it would not be the last. The immediate financial difficulty was due to the two-year involvement with the *Black Like Me* project. The *Sepia* series, "Journey Into Shame," had only resulted in the reimbursement of Griffin's actual expenses.

His series of articles had, as his wife Elizabeth often pointed out, "quite frankly, put *Sepia* on the national map," stirring tremendous interest from subscribers and new readers, as well as from the media and academia. The contract with his publisher did not include an advance on *Black Like Me*, because Griffin's account with Houghton Mifflin showed a negative balance – the sales of *Nuni*, his second novel published in 1956, had not covered the advance on *that* book. This was a pattern that would persist throughout most of his writing career. In fact, the bulk of income during the 1960s and up until the mid-1970s would be made as a lecturer not as a writer. Obviously, it was his growing reputation as the author of *Black Like Me* that generated the lecture tours. But never did he earn enough money from royalties to support family, astronomical medical expenses, and the ongoing cost of equipment and supplies (of which only a fraction would be defrayed by the sales of his photographs).

Griffin had an uncanny instinct for what made a story or a photograph or a musical composition significant, universal, beautiful – yet he had no business acumen, and often made poor financial decisions, trusting others with more expertise to take care of it. In some cases, he worked with people who shared his ideals and always he had the support of family and friends. There would be economic struggle during 1961, but several projects were in process, which related to the upcoming publication of *Black Like Me* – a paperback deal, translation rights from a dozen countries, interest in rights for film, stage, radio and television, and promotions for lectures, as well as Houghton Mifflin's advertising campaign for the book. But all these efforts would take time to reach fruition.

Meanwhile, he was finishing a final draft of his third novel, *Street of the Seven Angels,* a charmingly bawdy satire about censorship, which would not be published until 2003 – nearly a quarter century after his untimely death in 1980, at age 60.

After *Street of the Seven Angels,* he planned to continue writing an autobiographical work about his decade of sightlessness and eventual sight-recovery. This book would be published as *Scattered Shadows: A Memoir of Blindness and Vision,* in 2004.

The contract he had signed with Houghton Mifflin for *Black Like Me* would avail him of new openings, as he retained translation and film rights. But as for overseas negotiations, he had signed an excellent agreement with the Rosica Colin literary agency of London, which would represent him in the matter of British editions and translations throughout his lifetime. He had held on to these rights because little had been done by Houghton Mifflin for *Nuni* overseas – only a German edition had been published. The regional Smiths', publishers of his 1952 novel, *The Devil Rides Outside,* produced a text full of errors. The British edition from William Collins of London corrected these errors; the French and Dutch translations, as well as the successful paperback edition by Pocket Books, were all based upon the British text.

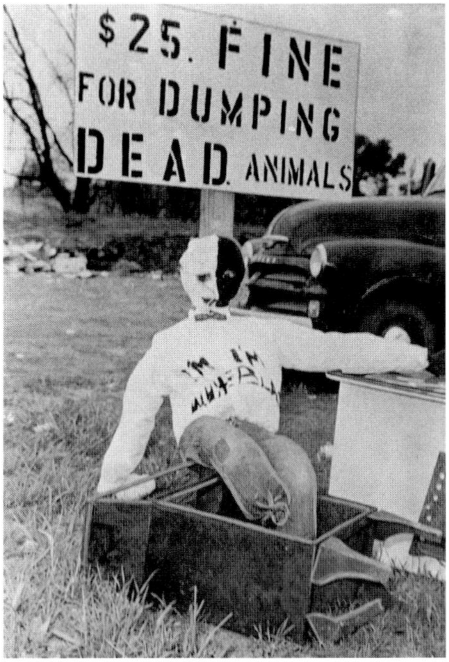

Before fleeing to Mexico, Griffin was informed that he had been "hanged in effigy" on Main Street in Mansfield, Texas (April 2, 1960). Griffin's name and a yellow streak were painted on the dummy's back. It was taken to the dump by the local constable. By the time a *Fort Worth Star-Telegram* photographer took this picture, someone had placed the dummy in front of this sign. Griffin later quipped that it was "not a very good likeness." Threats to Griffin and his family continued for several years.

Other basic problems beset Griffin during the summer of 1961. Not only had the Mexico exile exhausted their funds, but the family was also without their home. The cottage had been rented in their absence under the assumption they would not return to Mansfield. The family crowded into the home of Elizabeth's mother, Bess Holland. The rambling wood-frame structure in which Elizabeth had spent her childhood was just large enough to accommodate three adults and three children. With the rental income to help with some expenses, and the groceries being charged on Bess Holland's tab at a local market, they would survive.

However, this arrangement provided no space for a writing studio and, since he had not brought back the darkroom equipment, he was unable to develop prints, although he did continue shooting film. He solved the studio problem by turning a little wood frame storage shed into a workable space. The shed was about eighty yards from the Holland farm house, just behind the big barn. The shed's front windows looking out on a 30 acre pasture where goats, cows and horses ambled. Bess had used the shed for storing art supplies for classes she taught in Fort Worth.

With a loan from his parents, Griffin put in a floor, an air conditioner and a pot belly wood-burning stove. He lined the walls with mounted prints of the Tarascan images and portraits of his parents, wife and children. It was reminiscent of his old barn studio on his parents' farm, where he had written his novels during a decade of blindness. During June he wrote a spate of letters to old friends, catching up on the backlog of correspondence set aside while he remodeled the shed into a writing studio.

Early July brought good letters from friends and a much needed check for a thousand dollars from *Life* magazine for his "Terror in Mexico," published in their Spanish language edition. But there was also terrible news about Ramón Coté, the owner of the Villa Montana Restaurant in Santa María, who had been shot by communists; fortunately, the bullet had passed through the jaw and exited behind the ear, in such a way that he was neither killed nor paralyzed. As a result, the Tarascan men had armed themselves and patrolled the village. The Ellises had decided to move from Mexico back to Texas, and were building a home on the Gulf Coast near Galveston. The Shoemakers made a brief stop, on July 13, before returning to Mexico. Griffin loaded them up with letters for his Santa María friends, because mail was still being intercepted.

On July 17, Griffin returned to his *Journal* for the first time in two months. He spent the day proofing the typescript of *Street of the Seven Angels.* As usual, he had grave doubts about any book he finished, and shipped it without showing it to anyone.

Over the next few days, he helped Houghton Mifflin with promotional work. Press kits and galleys went out to Roland Hayes, Roy Wilkins, Leontyne Price, Marian Anderson, Sidney Poitier and James Baldwin; and to Ralph J. Bunche at the United Nations. Later, other prominent Black names were added, and copies were also sent to Flannery O'Conner, Lillian Smith, P.D. East and other white southerners.

Griffin requested that the press releases not include his place of residence and to say that he was not living in Texas. He wanted to keep his enemies guessing and he stayed away from downtown Mansfield. As for lectures, he said that he was "not prepared to speak in any of the hard-core Southern states," as he had received "many threats of assassination." He considered only

Atlanta as a possible exception, and wrote, "if this seems utterly fantastic in Boston, it is only too real in the South."

On July 27, Griffin laments in his *Journal* that, "I miss my darkroom equipment terribly. I keep making photos and feeling the frustration of not being able to develop and print them. I fritter the time, drawn to my major passion which is photography. I study a great deal – chemicals, emulsions, the lens combinations, and all the papers – all of the complex interrelationships that will allow for the finest end result: the print. Am now working with the microfilm-speed emulsions, very high resolution Adox Dokupan, and noting readjustments I will make."

Two significant events occurred on August 20. Griffin received an advance copy of *Black Like Me*, pleased with the "extraordinarily tasteful job." It was "good to leaf through and note names that are dear to me, names I revere in a text where I can honor them, perhaps, or at least make their message go to people who might otherwise miss it." His *Journal* entry concludes: "Always a strange moment, to see one's work printed into this format, complete – a year of labor that weighs less than a pound; and yet few pounds of any substance have produced the explosion this has, the repercussions, the changes in our life and status."

The second event was of his own making – an internal decision in the form of a letter to Decherd Turner. "I put my affairs in order, so that Decherd becomes my literary executor in the event 'they come and get him,' as Bess puts it."

> We begin the lugubrious business of seeking protection again, putting up blackout shades, so that if anyone comes up here at night they will not know if I am in – or at least cannot see to shoot me through the windows . . . . This kind of "sitting duck" uncertainty, the fear of a racist crackpot getting through, or a communist doing this so it can be blamed on the racists – fills me with renewed tenderness for my family, especially the children . . . and yet it was for them that I did it, and no matter what happens to me, I can at least know that what I did was an effort to make the world better for them, to give them hope of growing up in a less prejudiced climate, and therefore a less perverting climate.

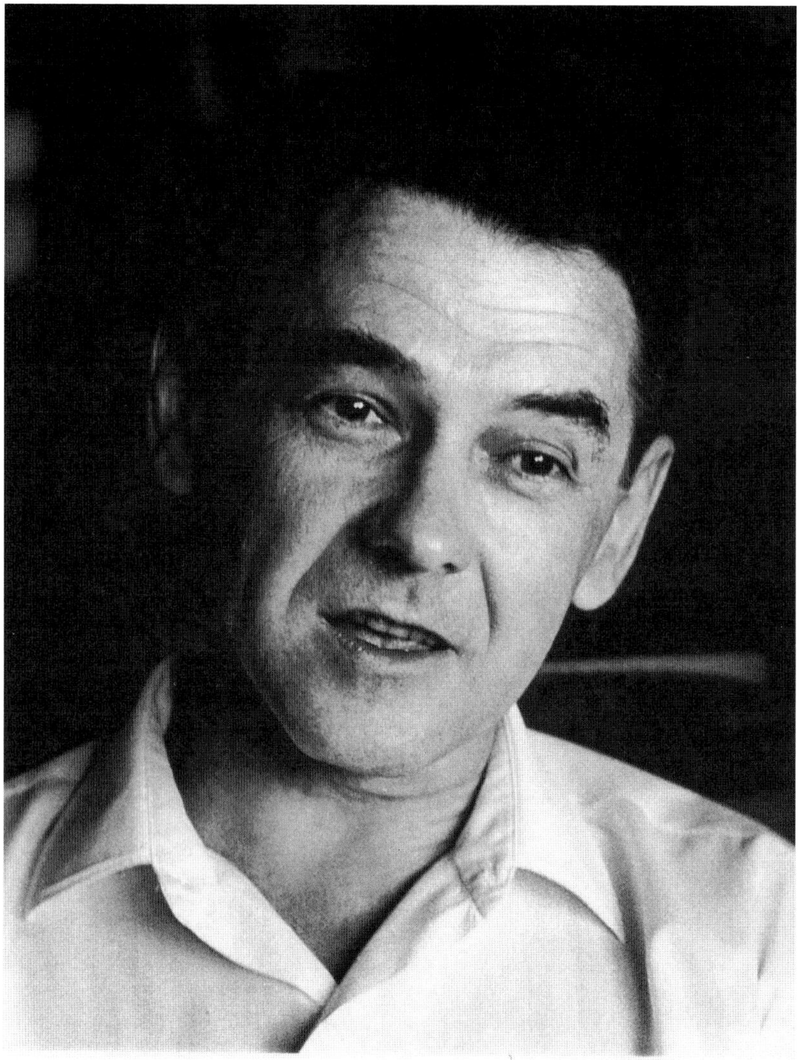

Griffin's 1964 portrait of Decherd Turner, Director of the Bridwell Library in the Perkins School of Theology at Southern Methodist University in Dallas. Turner, a renowned curator of rare books, was the first literary executor of Griffin's manuscripts.

His letter to Turner, written the same day as this *Journal* entry, informed Decherd that Paul Brooks of Houghton Mifflin was in receipt of a copy of what had been decided. "I wanted it clarified that you are to handle my unpublished works, which consist mainly of eight thick volumes of journals and many never-submitted short stories, plus a novel that has not been submitted, but that is near enough completion to require only a good editing job." The *Journal* at that point ran to 1,105 pages single-spaced typed pages. It would eventually run over 3,000 pages, of which only a fraction would find publication in his lifetime; he kept it in three-ring binders, which were not divided by year but simply filled to the brim. The novel he meant was *Passacaglia,* which he had drafted during the decade of sightlessness; it would never be submitted for publication, or even finished. The short stories were from that same period, most drafted before 1955, but only a few were published. The bulk of these manuscripts were still in the care of Luis Berbér in Mexico.

> There is a great deal in the journals that is obviously not meant for public view. You will know what should be submitted and what should not. . . . I should not like for you to consult with my family about what events or elements of the journals should be published, since their care for my memory would not allow them to judge properly. I feel that you alone would know me well enough to be the judge of this, and that you would not hesitate to publish whatever was of value, regardless of how it made me appear. . . but I feel that you, above all people, have the most complete knowledge of what my work tries to be, and would therefore be a better judge of what should be published than anyone else; which is why I should like all of this material to go through your editorial hands first. This letter will authorize you to take 10% in lieu of an agent's commission, which you will receive directly on all works that you handle and that are published in any and all forms after my death.

The next morning, Sunday August 21, Griffin felt a sense of closure. His literary estate had been put in order, and Decherd Turner was the right person for that massive, posthumous task. *Black Like Me* was about to be published, and *Street of the Seven Angels* was out of his hands. At that moment, he was right where he wanted to be – in the middle of drafting later chapters of *Scattered Shadows* – and with a confidence born of weeks of solitary writing. His great passion for photography, even though frustrated by the lack of a darkroom, had reached a level of technical expertise and artistic vision; and he was still studying elements of that craft with enthusiasm, shooting film for later development and scrutiny. The new shed studio had become a productive space despite its limitations. He looked forward to making this Sunday a day of dedicated continuity and creative accomplishment. But it was not to be.

"The poison starts," begins that day's entry. Before he had gone to the studio, he got a phone call "from a good friend, distressed by the tales that are being spread about me by those who would discredit the work, would nullify *Black Like Me*." He told the unnamed friend to ignore it, and he promised himself to do the same.

"I had prepared a good and enthusiastic day's work," he writes, "but this sours it – the interruption, the determination to keep utterly silent and not waste time defending myself, because it can drag on forever, and I have other work to do, and this keeps it from getting done." The poisonous lies could not kill the truth of the book; but they could devastate his resolve if he allowed it. It had come unbidden and, so too, its antidote. "A moment ago, Gregory came sleepily out to the studio, not yet awake from his nap, carefully wiped his bare feet on the door stoop and staggered in."

As the phone call had been an "interruption" to creative concentration, the innocent boy's unexpected arrival had interrupted Griffin's anger. "The thing that came clear is that I am not going to do this child's future any good except by working on my present book. The other is past. I have said everything I know to say – let them take it or leave it. I can spend months denying their lies, defending my work; and these months will be wasted, accomplishing nothing, not creating new works."

What "came clear" was not intellectual clarity, which was never far below the surface of his awareness, but a deeper emotional cauldron that was stirred always by personal attacks, by name-calling, by lies aimed at his credibility. But he could not let it go. He was still caught in a net of contradictions, in a struggle between prideful anger and the peace of self-purification in creating new work. "Yet, though I understand all of this, was prepared for it, a great heaviness lies on my chest, the desire to weep – why? – because my feelings are hurt . . . it's that childish." But at least he had been honest about his reaction, admitting that he had been hurt by the cruel attacks.

And he was wise to focus on the real essentials: "I have my manuscript, my typewriter, my paper, the silence of an August Sunday – nothing else really counts besides these" for the artist, who "must cast aside the stench, make use of the time to work and to love, avoid the temptation of defending one's good name . . . and yet, it is shattering. The instinct for self-preservation swells the glands, throws anger into the veins." That evening he visited his parents, who lived a dozen miles away from Mansfield in Venus, Texas, unwisely telling them about the local gossip, as if they would be immune. Thus, he "was astonished at his mother's anger, and regretted telling her." He tried to make light of it, to act as if all of it were "too ridiculous and amusing," but they were not laughing.

Late that night, listening to "the magnificent Bach Concerto for two violins," he reminisced about the music, yet felt the anger of internal contradictions.

> Now it is the slow movement of the concerto; magnificently beautiful and filling me with tenderness. I recall many years ago, when I used to play the two piano version of this work with my mother . . . and the marvelous joys of that compared to the bitterness and pain that I saw in her today. How I regret that my work, which should lead to beauty, leads to all this terrible venom against us. The hell of it is that this is turning her against humanity, embittering her, for she sees it in a degraded light in a way that few people are given to see it closely.

For the next three days, Griffin stayed at the Carmelite monastery south of Dallas (where he had been when his sight returned in 1957), keeping his promise to himself to continue with *Scattered Shadows* and to remain clear of phone calls and letters. Driving home from the monastery, he had "an extraordinary experience," which he wrote about in a letter to Father Stan, on August 26, 1961.

> . . . extraordinary because I had been suffocated by the stories going on about town, a nightmarish account of the good ladies' lynch parties against pornography . . . when what should I see looming up from a gigantic drive-in theatre screen, there to my left, in full view, but a group of completely nude women, blown-up to the giant screen, in the most ravishing Technicolor, cavorting in green waters. "Well," I told myself. "This did it. I've cracked up, lost my mind." I slowed down, sure that it was an hallucination (otherwise, there would be a whole stream of wrecked cars on the highway) and glanced cautiously. Yes, there they were, naked, wet, breasts and backs and hips. Badly shaken, but happy, I drove home and telephoned Decherd to ask him if I should have myself committed. He gently reassured me that it was some nature-studies picture that was causing a great stir "in good circles" – and that I had indeed seen what I had seen.

This passage about an unexpected, gigantic vision of nude women on display across the Texas prairie (in their "Renoirish loveliness") offers a taste of his comedic sense. Here it was intentionally silly – a combination of breast-sighting and leg-pulling for the entertainment of Father Stan, a liberated priest who enjoyed the harmless fun. The varied range of Griffin's comic vision is fully realized in *Street of the Seven Angels,* a satire about pornography and censorship in Paris – fictionally exploring the actual battle he had fought in defense of *The Devil Rides Outside.* In fact, some of the court dialogue in *Street of the Seven Angels* was adapted from the actual transcripts of the Michigan case, which eventually went to the Supreme Court where the novel was adjudicated as not being pornographic. Meanwhile, he avoided involvement in a cultural clash between the self-appointed censors and the defenders of free speech. He had "refused two such programs already, saying that I could not stand to debate 'police censorship' with grown men and women who accepted with indisputable fact that there was something intrinsically evil about sexual stimulation . . . a little item God created as a good." The real evils were racism and censorship, not freedom of expression and nudity.

By mid-September, Griffin had received several calls from Hollywood; three studios were interested in *Black Like Me* and another wanted to discuss the film rights to *The Devil Rides Outside.* He turned all the contacts over to George Levitan, publisher of *Sepia,* who was already negotiating with other studios. He also received a letter from Houghton Mifflin, informing him of New American Library's offer for the reprint rights to *Black Like Me*. They wanted to publish the paperback exactly one year after Houghton's cloth edition. The advance figure of $6,600.00 was small, but it had been the only offer. He accepted it, realizing that it would keep him from deeper debt.

On September 17, he wrote a brief entry in his *Journal,* after three weeks of silence. "Autumn is here, with cool, clear delicious days. Hard to stay inside and work. Many diabetic upsets, that leave me stupid and exhausted. They have never been so thoroughly ravaging before." Four days later, he experienced a violent insulin reaction – "a real thunderbolt that kept me in a coma for twelve hours and had all the appearance of heart attack complications." After two visits to his doctor and a battery of tests, he learned that there had been an "insignificant flutter" of the heart, but that the "devastating blood sugar imbalance had almost killed him."

On September 27, he was "physically sick, as though I had eaten ground glass – it was the Orinase to which I can never apparently accustom my system." He had survived again, but there would be continued adjustments to the insulin dosage. Also, he could not "escape the background preoccupation with death that always follows such an attack . . ."

During that same week, Hurricane Carla had struck the Gulf Coast with brutal force; the Ellises' recently-constructed beach house had been swept away. "Poor Bob and Rosa, they got out in front of the hurricane with nothing but the clothes on their backs. When they returned, they could find no trace of the house or lot (elevation had sunk four feet)." Ellis had "lost all of his canvases – and the recent ones were truly magnificent – he has developed into an unquestionably great painter." Elizabeth recalled the day the Ellises arrived in Mansfield after the storm. "They were still in shock and utterly exhausted. Rosa and I cried, and I could see that Bob was very shaken" – a fact that had struck her, because "he was always the most composed and relaxed person I'd ever known." All that was found after combing the beach was an iron skillet and a tiny piece of kitchen linoleum, which Bob "forlornly pulled out of his shirt pocket," Elizabeth said. The only fortunate relief was that the couple's three-year-old daughter, Erendira, had been with relatives. Elizabeth considered the Ellises her dearest friends and she loved them "as if they were the sister and brother I never had."

Ten days later, Griffin was suffering from the effects of the new insulin. "I feel I shall never really adjust to these insulin substitutes," he writes in his *Journal* on October 7. "Almost midnight, and I lie here in a stupor." He tried to pray, but "the prayers skitter off into nothing." He tried to write, but "it is full of dullness and errors." He wanted to remain awake until the medication wore off; he wanted coffee, but did not want to wake anyone at the house. He would have settled for music from the radio, as his record player was still in Mexico, but it was blaring the music of Offenbach.

> I write in this journal really to try to stir something, to come alive enough to do some work, to make myself think when my whole being drowses. This must be the way great age makes a man feel; the flesh dragging and hurting – the unwashed, uncomfortable animal. How odd and stupid Offenbach sounds on such a night. I listen to it with immense irritation, and wish the Offen were stricken from the name and I were hearing only Bach.

The Offenbach was followed by even lighter fare, which drove Griffin out of the studio toward the house to make a cup of coffee after all. "Walking in the intense darkness of October midnight, fragments of thoughts flickered: The body's weakness reminds man of self when the only hope is to lose self. . . .What happened to the God of tenderness? – the personal God so beloved by so many and once beloved by me? . . . but isn't that a fatal error of thought?" He filled a saucepan with water and watched it come to a boil. He put two teaspoons of instant coffee in a cup and poured in the water. Then milk and sugar, stirring the brew silently before drinking a few sips. He walked outside, where his questions turned into statements:

> God drove me to Him always with the most ineffable brutality. There has never been the sweetness in this relationship that I should have wanted to believe. How this would shock many, and rightfully. If I had been less stubborn, less recalcitrant, less smeared with the marrow of myself, He would not have had to badger

> and beat me into submission – into willing finally my submission because it was the only way. I came to God in utter defeat, and fell in love with God – coldly and passionately and tenderly – but late and without the habit of God; and now I fall away again and again, but with no loss of faith, only in my weakness, in stupidity, in numbness . . ."

Back at the studio, he wondered if these melancholic preoccupations had been caused by the medication. "How much of this is blood sugar and how much my own wantonness? God alone knows; I do not." He read the label on the medicine bottle. "It says on the bottle that this very thing is likely to happen, so why attach any spiritual connotations?" He drank the coffee before it turned cold.

More questions came as he typed and smoked. "Why this strange pride that feels hurt? What self-love to be humiliated (or disappointed?) by such things . . . Or rather what vicious habit of fastidiousness – ah, the habit of the pious." He paused to turn off whatever he was not hearing on the radio and lit another cigarette, watching the smoke rise. "If the effort were made, if the immense concentration could be summoned, the old warmth would return, the warmth of continual prayer, I try it."

During the pre-dawn silence of October 8, Griffin walked the floor with rosary in hand and intoned the scapular prayers. He turned out the lights and knelt to pray silently. He prayed until he was no longer aware of praying, and his anguish lifted. He flipped on the lights and returned to making notes with renewed energy and clarity.

> Much of religion – much of what we search for in religion and much of what we think we find in it – the peace and the delights are really the intervention of the ego, the escape into the ego we think sincerely we have cast out, overcome. We have escaped into the ego and keep building the ego, and then God sends us the agony, the deadness, the sensuality to clarify us and show us the immense duplicity of our whole religious stalemate.

Thus, in reaction to our paradoxical reality that animal and spiritual natures reside in human nature, we attempt to create an illusory escape from suffering. However, he writes, "the anguish is the thing to risk – it must be risked, and I see now, welcomed." Neither the "illimitable detachment of the angelic being" nor the sensate "plunge into the consoling pleasures" can be maintained. Both mechanisms attempt to deny the reality that life must die in order to be reborn into spirit. That mystery beyond language or silence, beyond logic or absurdity, Griffin believed, must live in one's abandonment in prayer.

To avoid the anguish of reality, "ego demands angelism" – but "one does not overcome the beast within him by simply being affronted and refusing to admit its existence; and yet this is the immeasurable temptation." The parallel delusion demands only the diversions in order to escape the agony of inhabiting a spiritual dimension.

But for Griffin, who believed that sanctity demands reality, one "must begin again to make the immense reconciliation of the contradictions (within the human mind, within our culture) between the beast and the angel. It will go with someone like me forever, starting over again with the pieces God has bashed into a mess."

Faith, then was the sole "virtue in a holocaust of error" – the simple "willingness to persevere." If one had limitless faith, according to Griffin, "the light never really goes out inside of self." And he considered that solitary light to be "that margin of safety."

He thought of music and tried the radio again, hearing the first movement of Mozart's C-minor *Concerto for Piano and Orchestra.* "Mozart comes to join me in a work to ravish the mind and soul with compassion and magnanimity."

It was an "immense reconciliation of the contradictions," that would once again bring him into balance.

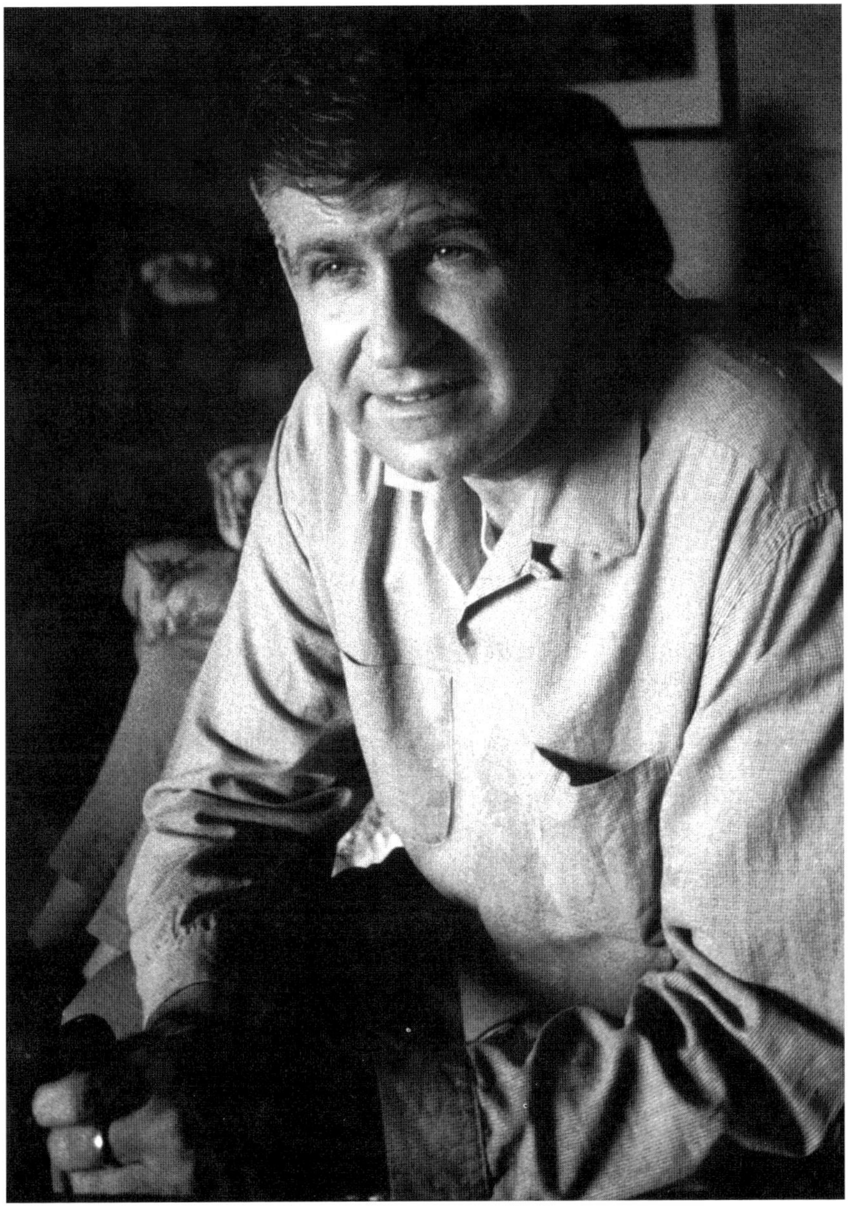

Portrait of John Howard Griffin by his younger son, Gregory Parker Griffin.

The Watch of the Dead

Legendary island of Janitzio, site of the annual Watch of the Dead ritual. The massive statue on the hill is that of José María Morelos, a Catholic priest who was one of the most brilliant leaders of a failed insurgency that attempted to drive the Spanish out of Mexico in the early 19th century. The city of Morelia is named after him.

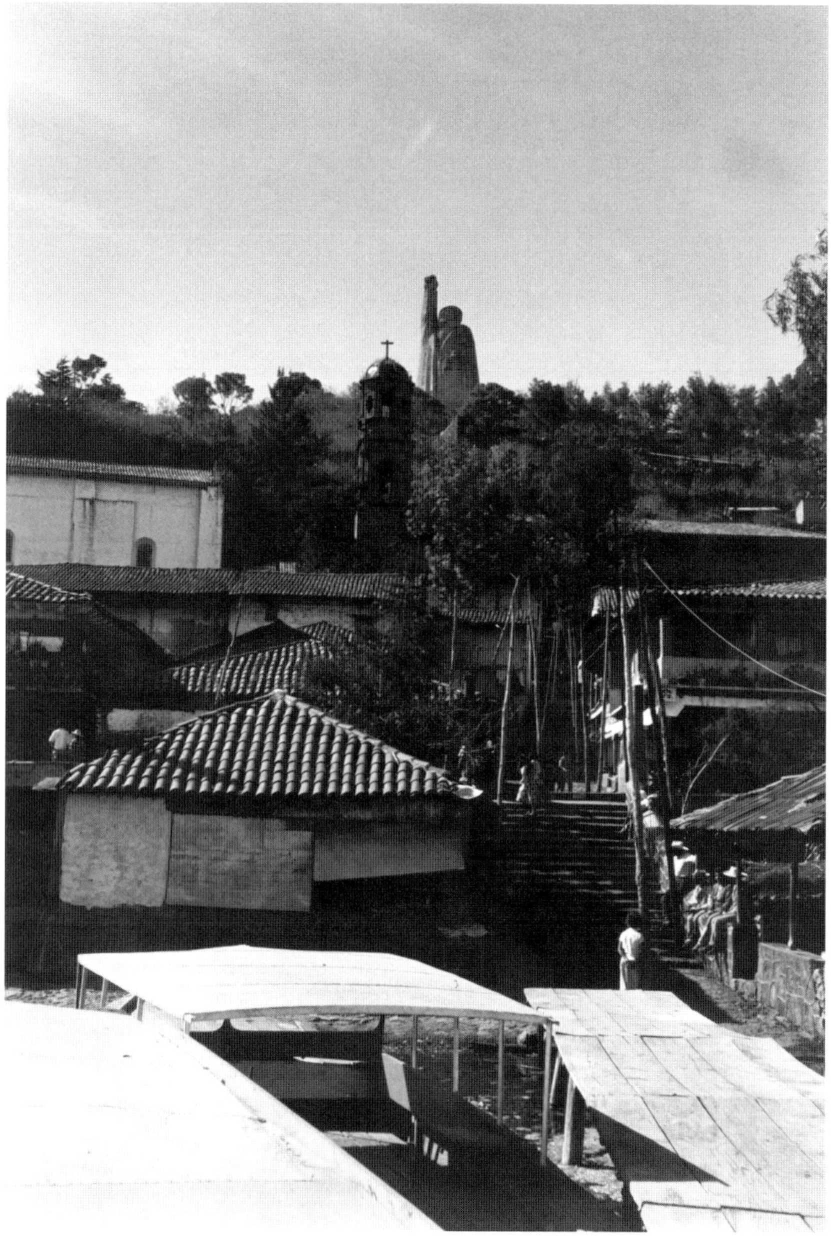

Every year on All Souls Eve, the Tarascan Indians celebrate the Watch of the Dead. They believe that the souls of deceased relatives return to visit them during the night.

Throughout the year, Tarascan families prepare for this reunion by saving for purchases of the finest beeswax candles, one candle to burn through the night for each deceased relative. Shortly before the event, they gather huge bouquets of yellow marigolds ("the flowers of the dead") and bake loaves of the bread for their dead loved ones.

These are carried on the night of the Watch to the *panteón* or burying ground where the family spends the night visiting with the spirits that return. Tarascan families look forward to this "reunion" as the major event of their year.

Although religious authorities in some areas have condemned the Watch, in the Tarascan country the belief is so powerful that the Church cooperates by offering services in conjunction with the rite.

Perhaps the most renowned of the Watches is held each year on the small island of Janitzio in Lake Patzcuaro at an eight thousand foot altitude in the Sierra Tarascas. The island can be reached only by boat from the mainland. Lake Patzcuaro provides an abundant supply of the famous white fish, *pescado blanco,* and most of the island's inhabitants are fishermen.

In 1960 I made a request, through officials, to attend the Watch of the Dead for the purpose of photographing the rite. I was informed that my request might be considered, but that flash photography was strictly prohibited. The islanders were sick of the yearly invasion of tourists with their liquor and flashbulbs and curiosity.

This year, no guests were to be allowed on the island. I assured the officials I would photograph discretely and without any supplementary light. Permission was granted, but the final decision would be up to the islanders themselves. They might very well refused to let me ashore.

I doubted that I would ever set foot on Janitzio that evening, for as I took the boat from the mainland city of Patzcuaro, I saw other boatloads of visitors moving toward the island. Surely not all of them could have received permission. In early dusk, Janitzio rose up from the water, a giant statue of Morelos standing like a cathedral spire at the island's peak. In the distance, on all sides, mountains loomed hazily.

Tarascan women on the island of Janitzio, with Lake Patzcuaro in the background.

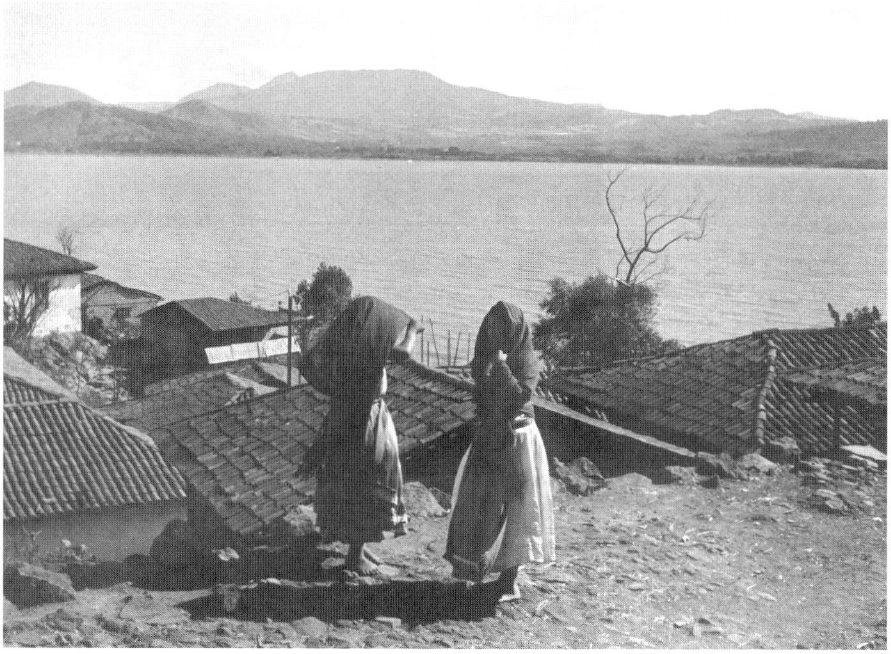

At the shaky wooden docks I learned that the orders against visitors had been rescinded. Local police let us pass one by one after making certain we did not carry flash equipment or liquor and with a polite admonition that we make ourselves no more obnoxious than necessary.

I climbed the steep cobblestone street toward the church halfway up the hill in the last dim light of dusk. Candles had been lighted in some of the houses, the doors of which opened directly onto the narrow street. The fragrance of smoke from supper fires mingled with the beginning chill of the rarefied mountain air.

Along the winding cobblestone ascent, stone benches had been constructed into the wall edging the root. Islanders walked in the soft light or sat on the benches, smoking their pipes and talking. I saw no vehicles of any kind on the island, and certainly no roads that could accommodate an automobile. Men walked or rode burros.

I pushed open the heavy doors of the church and heard them creak shut behind me. People knelt at the Benediction in the candlelit interior. In the center, as though it were a bier, stood a large stack of loaves of "bread of the dead" surrounded by bunches of "flowers of the dead" with lighted tapers at each corner. They had been brought to be blessed. Shawled women and children and hatless men knelt, dark masses in a flickering light, absorbing the odor of incense.

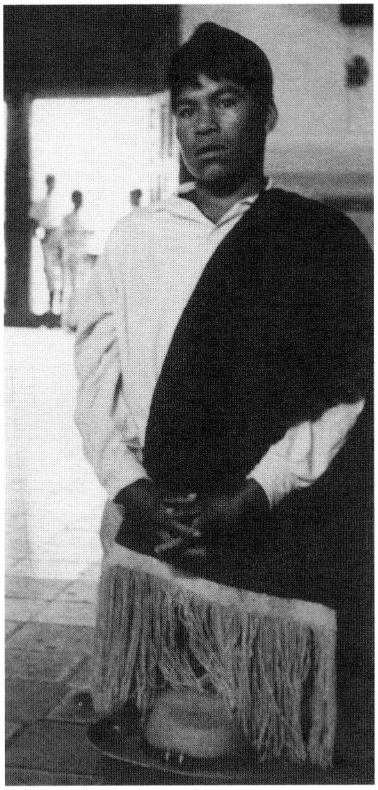

A young Tarascan villager kneeling in church before the Watch of the Dead ritual.

After the service, I visited a moment with the local priest, an affable and talkative man. He advised me to go now and get supper. "Eat as much as you can," he said. "The night is long and it gets very cold. No more food will be available once the Watch starts," he added. He told me that most visitors leave shortly after midnight and repeated again that if I planned to stay the whole night I must fortify myself with food.

The cafe was a small square structure, open to the air, with benches and counters on all four sides. Tarascan women in their long black skirts and shawls stood over the charcoal braziers, surrounded by smoke, and cooked the *pescado blanco* along with smaller sardine-like fish from the lake. We had a choice of the smaller or larger fish and soft drinks. I ordered a platter of the silvery minnows, quick fried in a sweet oil, and a glass of lukewarm lemonade.

The fish, caught only that afternoon, were served crisp and hot in huge portions. The visitors knew that we were eating one of the world's finest and most delicate foods. We lingered, absorbing the warmth from the braziers while the cold wind off of the lake chilled our backs.

After supper I carried my cameras up the mountainside to the *panteón* through a high stone arch topped by a cross. I was mystified to see no grave markers, not even a mound to indicate where bodies were buried. The earth was perfectly flat, covered with loose sandy soil pocked by thousands of bare feet.

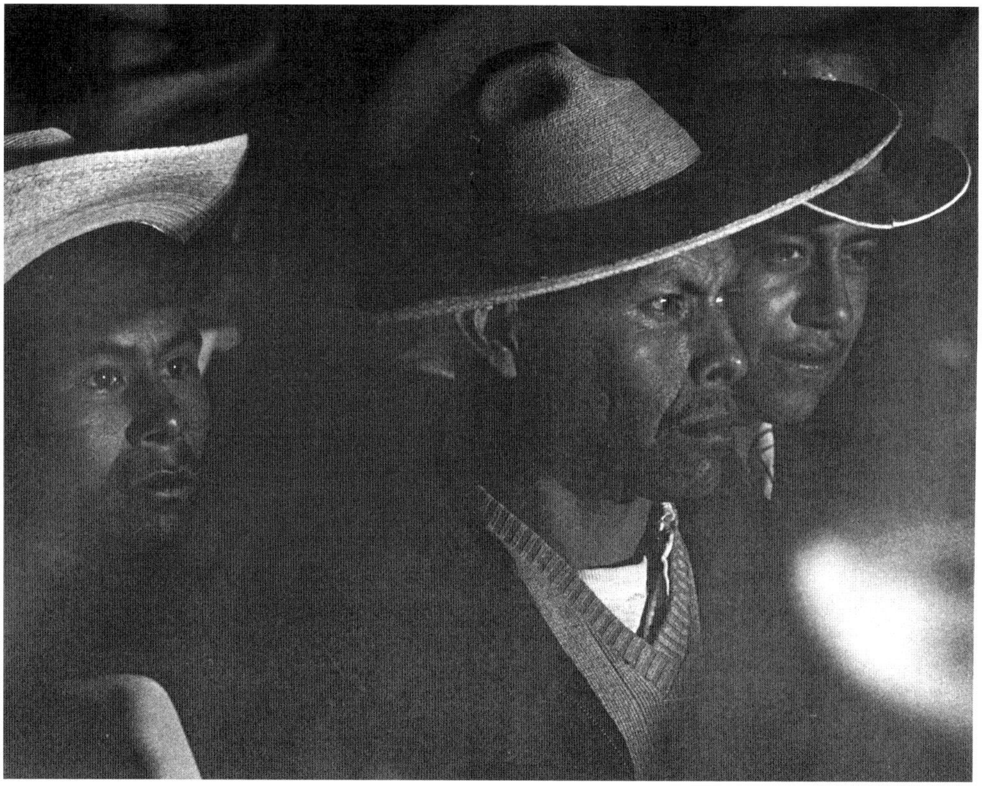

Tarascan fisherman on the island of Janitzio during the Watch of the Dead. This photograph was published in *The John Howard Griffin Reader.*

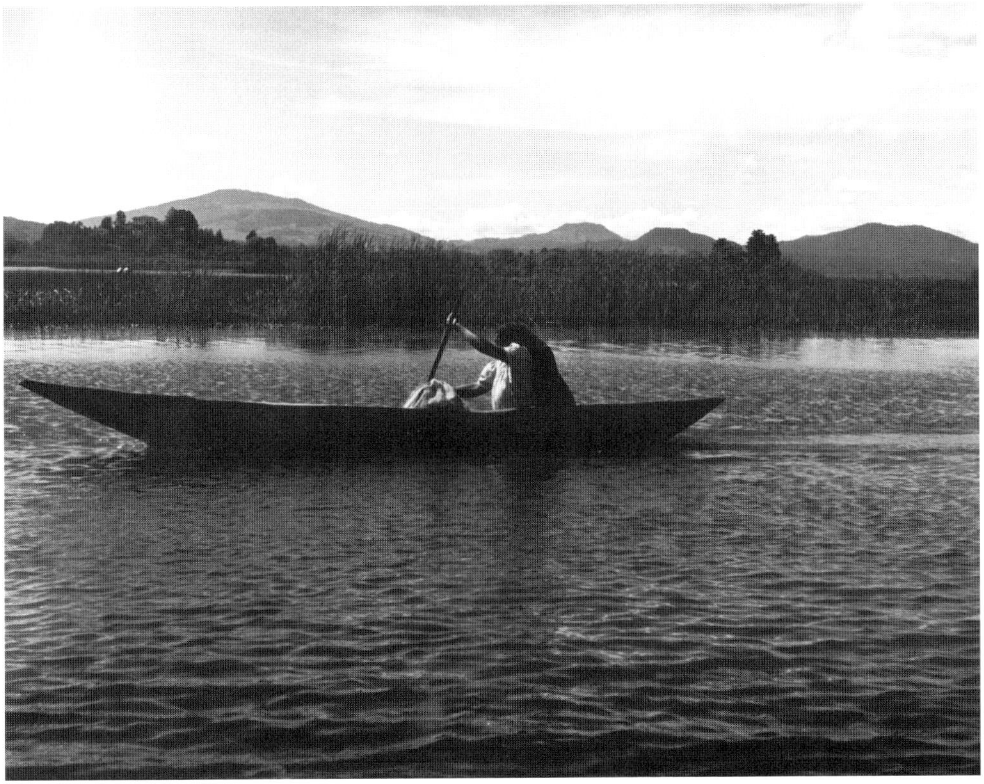

Tarascan woman rowing on Lake Patzcuaro, toward the island of Janitzio. This photograph was published in a booklet about the Singing Boys of Mexico.

But apparently the inhabitants knew the exact locations where their relatives were interred for already they were setting up the tall beeswax candles and spreading out the flowers and foods for the dead. If a man had a fondness for some particular food or drink, that was provided; if the deceased were a child, fruits and toys were spread out on the grave or placed on racks. When the spirit returned, it would see that its favorite foods had been prepared in offering and would be happy.

Within an hour, thousands of candles and a few small fires glowed against the rugged face of the cliff. Men, women and children sat quietly around their clusters of candles to await the return of the spirits. An almost festive and serene hush hovered over the crowded *panteón*.

In an area where until recently they suffered a fifty percent infant mortality rate, I sensed the overwhelming tenderness of parents, anticipating the visit of their dead children, certain they would come.

I walked quietly, another mere shadow in the candlelit night, photographing silently, though I made no attempt to conceal my actions. Nowhere was I rebuffed. The Tarascans, a people of the greatest natural dignity and beauty, asked only that we not openly intrude.

Then one man used a flash. A rumble of protest rose from the crowd. He used it again and then no more. Presumably he was escorted away. For an hour I made no more photographs. The mood had become strained because of the flash equipment.

Around ten that night, I was seated on the ground near an elderly solitary Tarascan lady who sat before two large candles. She apparently guessed my reluctance to photograph after the flash incident.

"Do you want to photograph me?" she asked quietly.

"May I?"

"Of course."

In the candlelight I was overwhelmed by the physical beauty of the islanders. I recalled reading that one of the chroniclers with the Cortez expedition had spoken of the Tarascans as "by far the most beautiful of the Indian tribes we have encountered."

The priest had been correct. Shortly after midnight most of the visitors succumbed to the deep cold and returned to the mainland. Only a handful of "outsiders" remained. One couple, a Mexican anthropologist and his wife, offered me a cup of coffee from their thermos. We sat on the stone bench and the scientist asked about photographing without flashbulbs. I explained my equipment to him between chattering teeth.

I would never have thought that such cold was possible in this semi-tropical climate, but the air, still and calm, was soon near the freezing point. My hands became so numb I could hardly manipulate the cameras. Mothers wrapped smaller children in blankets and cradled infants near the fires. Some of the children slept but a surprising number remained soberly awake. I heard not one complaint.

Shortly after two in the morning the quiet murmur of conversations hushed as a woman's sobbing shocked the atmosphere. She was quickly quieted and the conversations resumed.

"What was it?" I asked the anthropologist.

"I guess she felt the presence of her dead child," he said. "She was over-come for a moment. That's unusual. I've never heard anyone cry out during The Watch of the Dead. The mood of these visits is always one of deep peace, almost never anguish."

Shortly before dawn, while the night was black, the priest arrived to celebrate Mass on an open-air altar. The islanders, without changing positions or moving from their places, gave the Mass responses, their voices rising from the candlelit darkness on all sides to reverberate against the cliffs and float bodiless into the cold night air as though in some widely diffused reedy orchestration. As Mass ended, dawn began to give us the shape of the cliff and silhouette of the gnarled tree far above us. The water and distant mountains emerged in monochrome reality.

Then, without seeming to move, the islanders were quickly gone from the *panteón*. With the first light of dawn the spirits had left.

Soon the fragrance of coffee and smoke from their breakfast fires drifted to us. A few of us remained to watch dawn infuse the landscape with luminous pinks and oranges softened by white mists that clung to the lake. I walked about, trying to forget the pangs of hunger. No debris, no candle or bread crust or flower petal remained to give evidence of the Watch. The pocked sand stretched clean and deserted.

We discussed the Watch, needing to hear our voices in the brilliant stillness. The Mexican anthropologist said he had heard one mother murmur

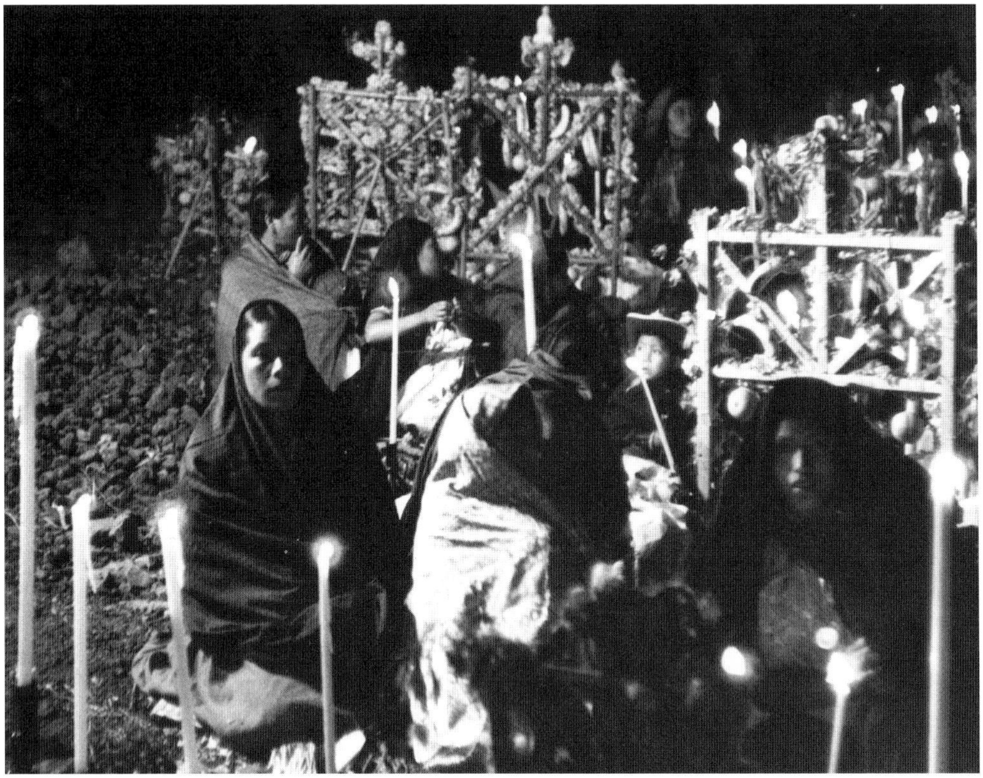

Tarascan families honoring deceased loved ones with offerings and lighted candles at the Watch of the Dead.

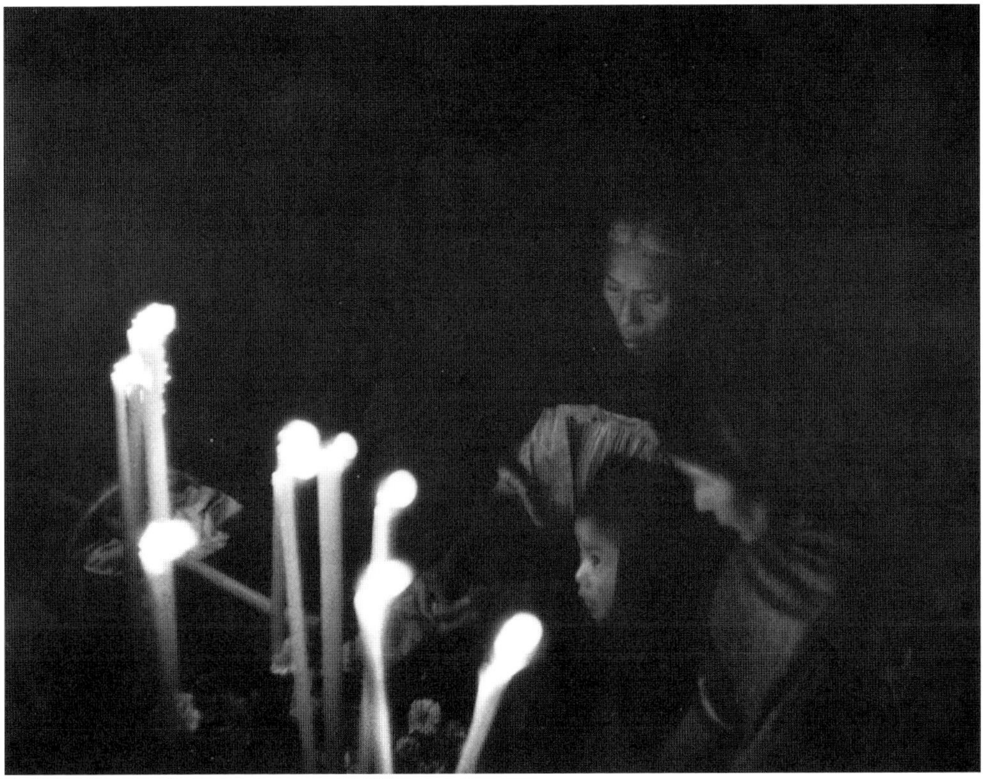

Mother and child during the Watch of the Dead. This photograph, like all of Griffin's, was taken with available light – in this instance, thousands of candles.

that she was sorry it was over and remarked that the visit with her son had been sweet.

The sudden clear clangor of bells from the church attracted our attention. Those who had not attended the predawn Mass were being called to the regular morning Mass in the church. No boats appeared on the lake. They would rest today, the men who had attended the Watch.

Then we heard the approaching babble of voices. Three young girls walked through the arched entrance to the *panteón*, giggling and chattering as they adjusted their long scarves over their heads and shoulders. They crossed the area leisurely and strolled up toward the top of the island. Their appearance, their laughter dissipated the final haunting resonances of the Watch of the Dead.

Passion at Tzintzuntzan

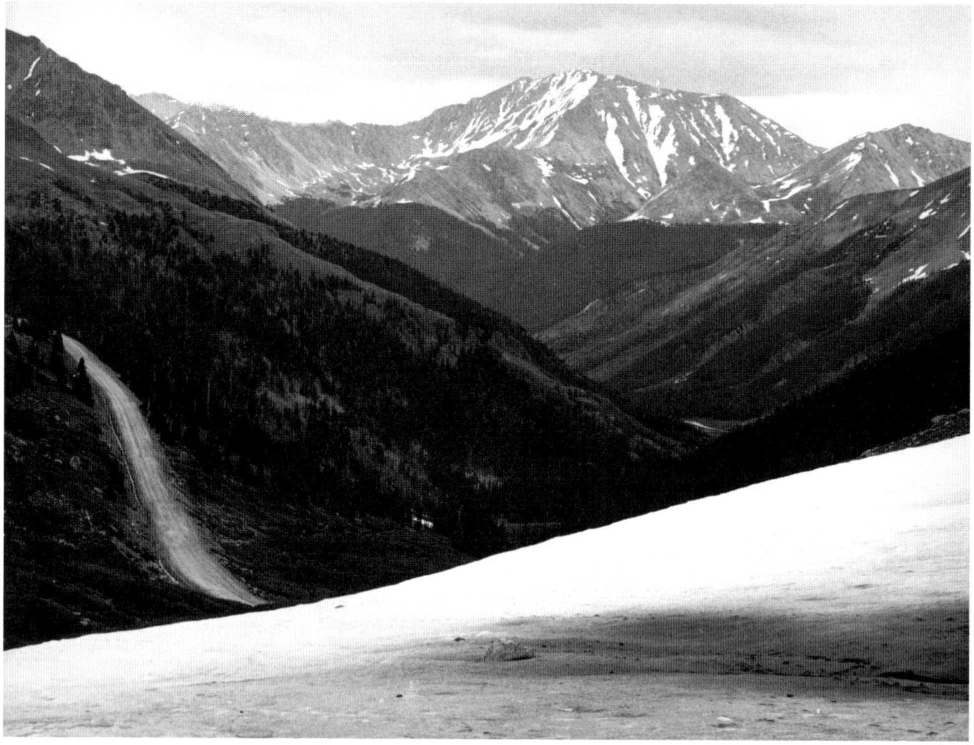

Sierra Tarascan mountains between Morelia and Tzintzuntzan in the State of Michoacán, Mexico. The highest peaks of the range reach altitudes over 8,000 feet.

Tzintzuntzan, once the capitol city of the Tarascan empire, is now a quiet village on the highway between Morelia and Patzcuaro in the Mexican state of Michoacán. It lies near the shore of Lake Patzcuaro in a valley high in the Sierra Tarascas mountains.

Each year the people relive the events of Holy Week in the streets and compounds with a sense of reality that becomes almost hallucinatory.

The villagers prepared silently for the Passion when I arrived on Holy Thursday morning. A hundred yards off the main highway, stone walls enclose the six-acre compound of this sixteenth-century Franciscan Monastery of Solitude. I entered through the arched gates and walked past giant olive trees planted by Spanish Franciscans four hundred years ago. Near the back wall, the original monastery stands, as do the original church and a more recent one.

An elderly priest, Padre Ernesto Tovar, occupies the monastery's crumbling magnificence alone now. I found him seated under cloister arches in a courtyard brilliant with flowering trees and shrubs. A barber shaved the octogenarian priest and trimmed his white stubble of hair in preparation for the events to come. Father Tovar graciously confirmed our prior agreement that I was to photograph the Passion as part of a proposed cultural history of the Tarascan civilization. "I have told my people to cooperate with you," he said.

"May I look around," I asked, nodding toward the abandoned upstairs portion of the cloister.

"Of course. This is your home."

I wandered through the second floor cells and corridors, my feet stirring dust. Odors of stone and age surrounded me. Ghosts of the past hovered over the ruin, telling me that this was once a center of Franciscan learning where friars copied manuscript books on mathematics, philosophy and theology; where they painted frescos on the courtyard walls depicting the Sacraments.

Drawn to these ghosts, I felt glaringly out of place and time as I opened my case of splendid cameras with their precision optics, set up tripod and photographed the peeling frescos.

It was soon done, but I could not leave. I turned at the stairway and walked back down one of the corridors to the last cell at the end. I seated myself on a stone niche carved as a kind of chair against the wall and looked out the hole that had once been a window. Mountain peaks rose in the background. In the foreground below, children played beneath tall jacarandas that were covered with blue blossoms.

I sensed some strangeness. Something was not natural in the sights and sounds. It became clear. The children made no sound. Nothing made any sound. Birds were hushed. Except for breeze-stirred leaves, silence brooded over the land. Christ was away, beyond sight and sound, on the Mount of Olives.

Guards, dressed in white, with faceless blood-red hoods and belts, rode their horses through the narrow village streets below my window. They searched for Christ. The horses' muffled footsteps, like the sounds of heartbeats, deepened silence rather than broke it. Occasionally, in the distance, an oboe-like Tarascan shepherd horn sounded its plaintive call, flooding the sunlit countryside with melancholy.

Terror insinuated itself implacably into the atmosphere despite the brilliant light, the profusion of flowers and the crowds of Tarascans who streamed toward the compound from neighboring villages. The genius of the terror sprang from the silence, the strange shepherd call in the distance, the growing awareness that Christ, invisible to us, was being searched down.

Outside, I sat on the church terrace to change the film in my cameras. Across the compound, Barabbas, in sackcloth and chains, and Judas – both wearing ghastly pink masks – strutted among the olive trees. Judas waved a long black sack of coins. Children ran from the two villains. Soon, most of the children had gathered around me. We spoke in smiles, making no sound. Their handsome faces shone with curiosity about my cameras, but they were too courteous to examine them overtly.

A brief flowering of sights and gasps caused me to look up from my work. Judas and Barabbas sauntered toward me. Since their designs were obviously on me, the children did not run. The two elbowed their way arrogantly through the crowd. Barabbas rattled his chains and gestured in a mute plea for money. I looked questioningly at the lad beside me. He stared soberly, giving no hint what I should do.

Barabbas became more insistent, placed one hand on my shoulder and pushed me back on the ground. He tried to force a bottle of tequila into my mouth. Grit rubbed into the back of my head. The pink-masked man held my cheeks with one hand and rammed the corked tequila bottle against my mouth with the other. We struggled in silence. I pushed him back, finally, and reached for my wallet. When I took out the peso for Barabbas, Judas reached down and snatched a five-peso note. Both hurried jauntily away.

The children eyed me with expressions of sorrow and reproach. The youngster nearest me whispered in my ear that it was evil to give money to Judas. I whispered, apologizing but making the point that I had not given it, Judas had stolen it. Nevertheless, they made me feel the guilt of being one of those who paid Judas to betray Christ. I had contributed my part of the thirty pieces of silver. To exonerate myself in their eyes, I decided to go take the money away from Judas.

The crowd followed as I hurried after the two men. They were busy terrifying children under a large tree near the old original Church of Solitude and did not notice our approach. By gesture I demanded my money. Barabbas grabbed the back of my neck and shoved the tequila bottle against my lips again. Judas held his sack of coins high and pushed against me with his free hand. When I would not leave them, Judas caught my arm and guided me into the empty church. He pointed to a chalked sign which said that any money given to any of the actors of the Passion would go to the church. I nevertheless made him take the five pesos from his bag and put it into the alms box.

The children no longer regarded me with fear. I had corrected the error. I was back on the "right side." The hypnotic effect of time and place became apparent. We were so involved that I found it difficult to realize that this was essentially an *ad libitum* play. I felt split, part realizing this was the twentieth century, part eerily involved in the event two thousand years ago. This latter was so predominant that I was astonished to feel anything so banal as hunger or thirst or other needs while the greatest event in Christian history advanced toward its climax.

Yet hunger was there, and heat and thirst. A thick, reddish dust, stirred by the crowds, hung over the compound. Vendors had set up stands under the trees. They sold melon slices that were covered with crawling brown bees; and hard pastry sandwiches topped with a pink icing that represented the blood of Christ. I ate a crumbly sandwich and drank tepid apple cider.

Awareness of Christ permeated the compound, and yet we were as the crowd must have been then – wondering where He was. Soldiers prepared Christ's cell, a dark cubbyhole in the church wall. Padre Tovar told me that

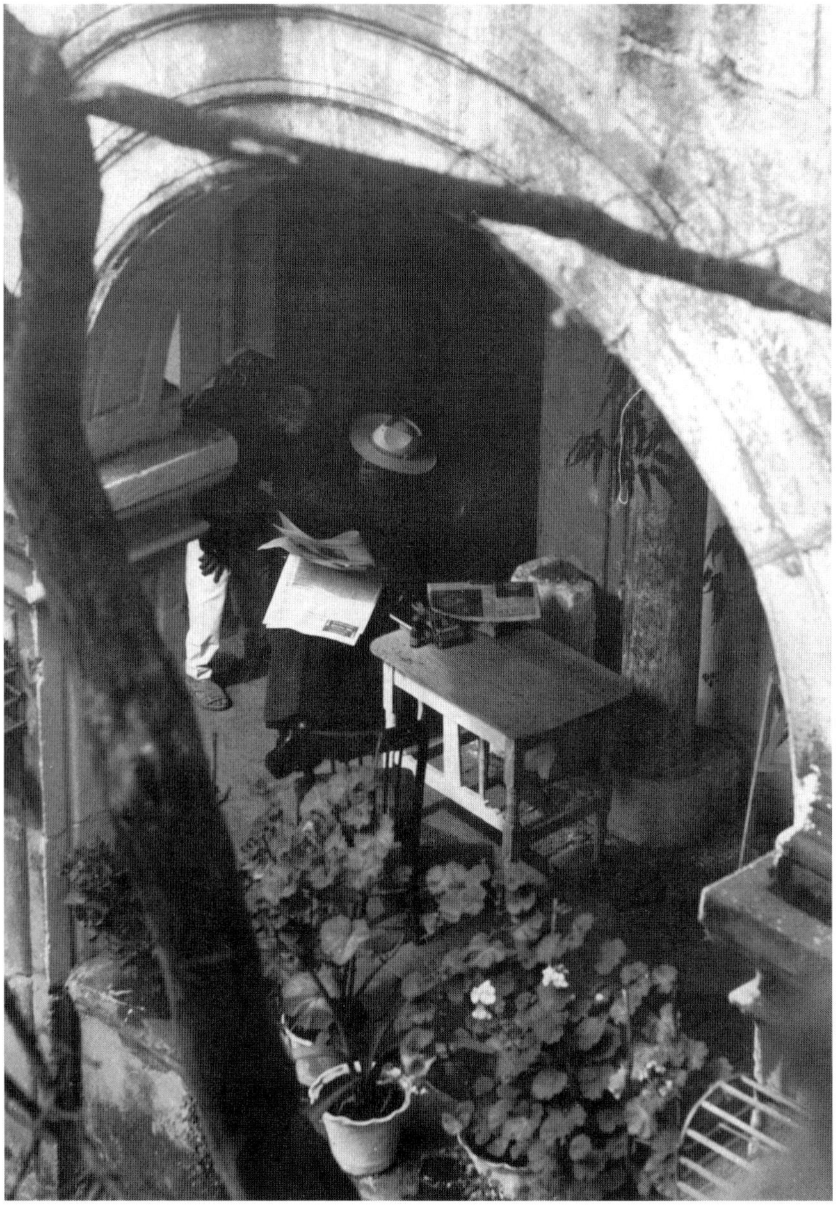

Padre Tovar, the rector (and the last occupant) of the Franciscan monastery at Tzintzuntzan, known as the "Monastery of Solitude."

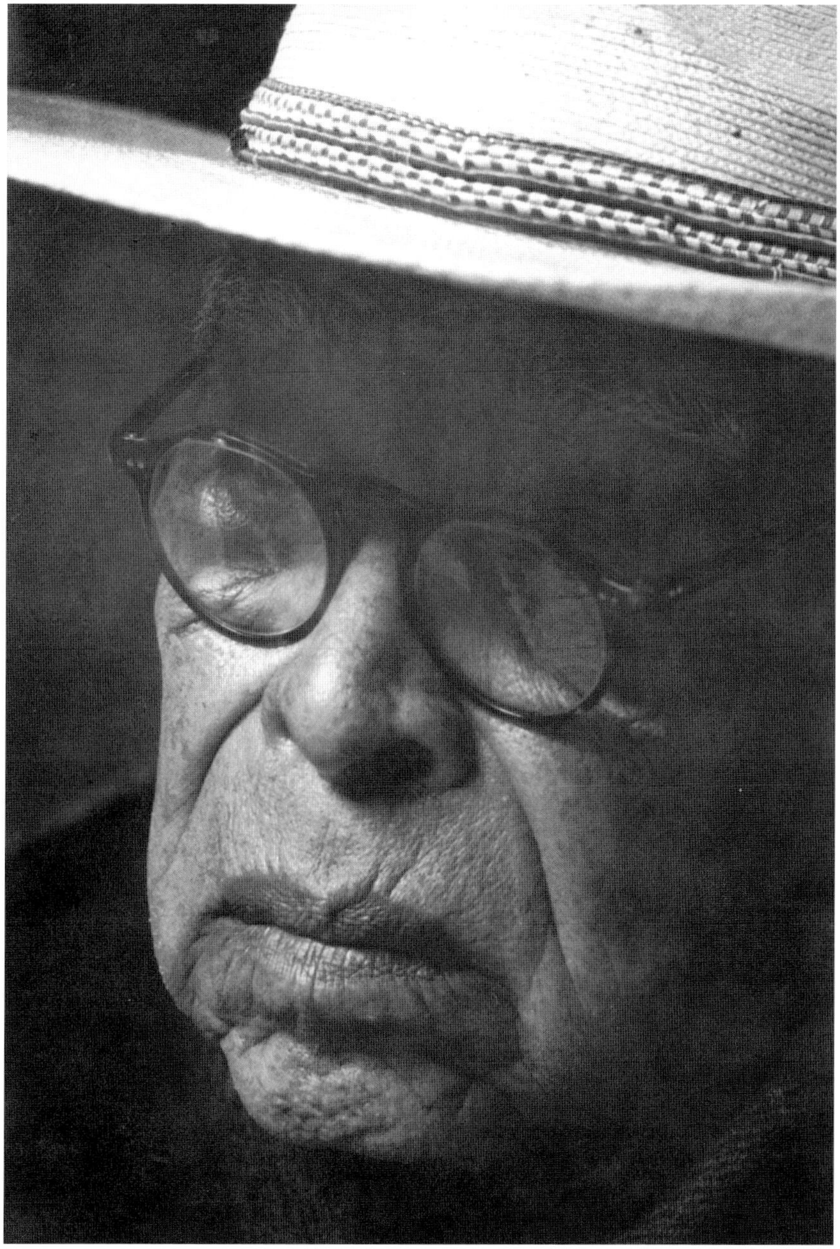

Portrait of Padre Ernesto Tovar taken by Griffin in 1961. This photograph appeared in *The John Howard Griffin Reader.*

Christ's role is always a voluntary one. Each year a young Tarascan offers to suffer the ordeal. He would, the priest explained, go through all of Christ's physical agonies, with the exception of the final sacrifice when the human is rushed to a hospital and a famous *Cristo* with movable arms and legs is nailed to the cross.

This year's volunteer would spend the night standing in his cell, without food or water. The next day he would undergo Christ's agony. About half of the Christs actually died from the ordeal, the priest stated. The town's citizens paid the hospital bills of those who survived.

Late in the afternoon, guards pushed and shoved Christ mercilessly into the compound. We had not witnessed the kiss of Judas, as the crowd two hundred years ago had not witnessed it. It was strange to see it as the people must have seen it rather than as the Gospels recount it. We glimpsed the magnificent figure of a young Tarascan Christ, his hair long and matted, his face radiant with dread and expectation.

I heard English being spoken and glanced around, surprised to hear words in any language after the hours of silence. An American family had come to witness and photograph the event. Their twelve-year-old son moved to my side, eyed my cameras, showed me his own fine instrument and began to shoot pictures.

When the guards and Christ were within a few feet of us, they halted. A guard slipped a crown of viciously real thorns onto the Christ's head, carefully, gently. With a dull pop the thorns pierced the flesh and blood poured down into the Christ's face. The young Tarascan did not wince. He was steeled for the torture to come. But the rest of us winced, though there were no outcries.

"That's enough for me," the American mother said, taking her son firmly by the arm and guiding him away. They left quickly.

I think it was not the cruelty of the scene so much as the incredible illusion that this man was Christ, that we were participating in the real Passion, that this went far beyond the niceties of play-acting. As such it was an unbearable agony for the spectator as well as for the victim. It shriveled the heart with dread.

Following the trial and condemnation, they dragged the Christ to the small cell and locked him up for the night. Red-hooded guards with faceless masks stood watch behind their spears. Some of the crowd remained outside the cell door, praying. Others went into the two churches and knelt in the barren candlelit interiors. Dogs howled in the distance. The Tarascan shepherd horn sent its desolate call through the moonlit night. We remained suspended in time, waiting for the hours to pass, some kneeling like frozen statues in the church, others in the courtyards among the trees. Some women sat against the high compound walls, cradling their sleeping children who were wrapped in woolen shawls against the chilly night.

At midnight I walked toward the monastery where I intended to sleep on the floor of one of the cells. But someone had locked the doors. I moved toward a lighted house in town to ask if I could rent a room. A small group gathered under the light, full of concern. But no, there were no hotels in Tzintzuntzan, they explained. I asked if I could sleep in the jail. No, it was filthy. With many apologies, they found a mat for me, regretting that it could not be a bed; and I arranged to sleep on the floor in a spare room of a neighboring house.

The next morning, the family served me breakfast of scrambled eggs, tortillas and coffee in a beautiful old kitchen that opened out to a courtyard crowded with flowers and children. The morning was overcast and misty. While eating, I watched through the window as barefoot Tarascan girls, with shawls over their heads, walked past in the street.

I tried to imagine how it must have been here when Tzintzuntzan was the capitol of the Tarascan empire and the home of its emperors – a city of one hundred thousand. The small village of five hundred gave little hint of its important past.

Across the street, the Tarascans had sacrificed in one day six hundred slaves, as an act of mercy, to keep them from falling into the hands of the Spanish conquerors. Here, the Spanish "butcher" Guzmán had tortured the last of the Tarascan emperors to make him give up his people's treasures. Then they had him dragged through the streets tied to the tail of a horse until he was almost dead, and publicly burned him at the stake as a warning to the Tarascans never to hide their valuables from the Spanish. All of this was done, they said, for "the greater glory of God and Spain."

Here, too, the Franciscan Fray Juan de Cordura wrote scathing denunciations of his fellow Spaniards for their degradation of the Tarascans, repudiated the Spanish and lived out his life with the Tarascans. "If only they had sent just

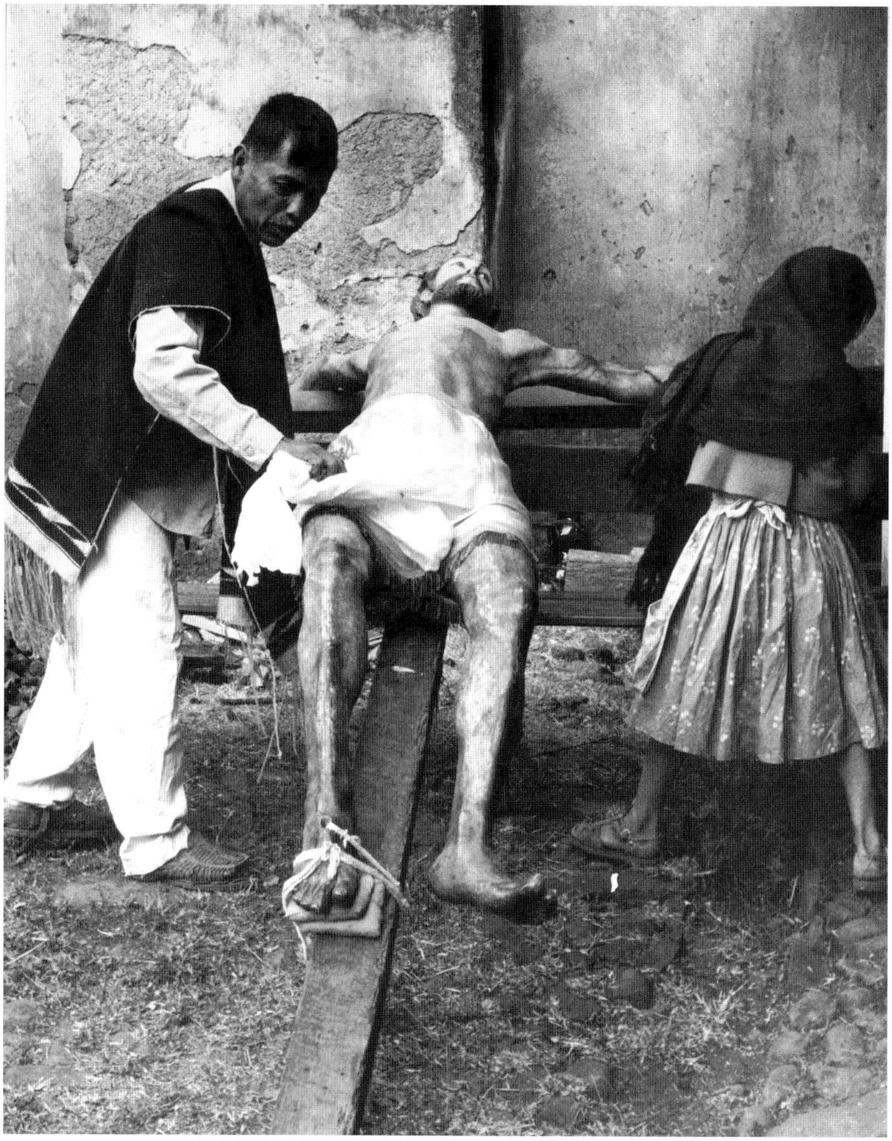

Villagers cleaning the wooden *Cristo* before the Passion begins in Tzintzuntzan.

the Franciscans and left the others in Spain," the Tarascans lament even today.

When I stepped out into the street, the sun had broken through clouds. The air was fragrant with wood smoke from breakfast fires. The radiance of early morning intensified the unspeakable horror of the events that were destined to take place that day.

I entered the old church as a group of men were carrying the famed life-size statue of the crucified Christ out a side door into a courtyard. I watched them deposit the figure gently, with its upper portion on a sawhorse. They began dusting it off, and wherever they dusted, they kissed the body. A large,

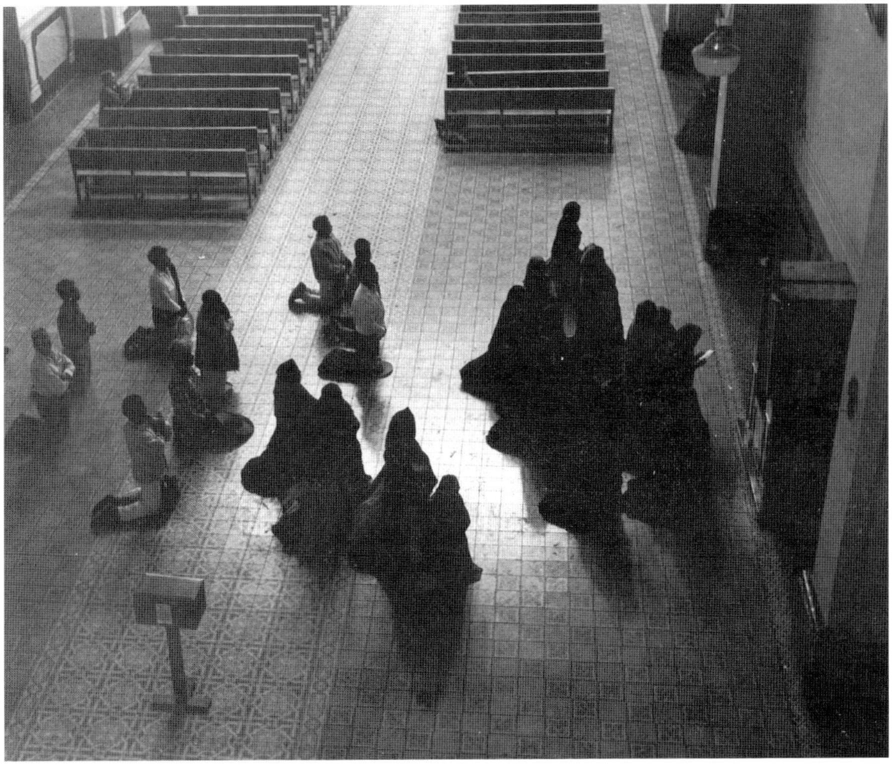

Villagers praying in the church after the Passion of Christ in Tzintzuntzan.

elderly, tough-looking matriarch sent them away and took over the work. When she bent over to kiss the body, I prepared to photograph. She commanded me not to make any photographs. I explained to her that I had Father Tovar's permission, that I did this in reverence, to show the world how the people of Tzintzuntzan observed Holy Week.

The matriarch gave a snort of disgust and said I would have to pay her to photograph the Christ.

"Why?" I asked. "Does the Christ belong to you any more than He does to me?"

This amused her. The old matriarch seemed to love a good, slightly insulting argument. "You pay or you don't photograph. The money goes to the church."

"I intend to give Padre Tovar a contribution," I said. "I certainly don't intend to pay for every shot as I take it. And when I do pay, I'll give it to the priest, not some old woman."

We understood one another, and liked one another. She almost smiled at the quality of my insult.

"Then you don't photograph," she announced grandly. "Why don't you just edify me by going to some other land?"

"Why don't you just edify the world by bending down and kissing the Christ so we can show the world what a pious person you really are."

"Pooh – never – not without money."

"All you want from your relationship with Christ is money. That is not good. No, I wouldn't photograph you at all. Will you step away, so I can photograph the Christ?"

She gazed at me through slit eyelids, repressing a smile. "Oh, hell, what do you want me to do?" she asked grudgingly.

"Now you are being amiable," I laughed. She shrugged good-natured defeat. I approached close to the head of Christ, which was at the level of my hips on the sawhorse. "Bend down and kiss the figure," I said.

"How?" Her eyes glinted, with no trace of malice left in them.

I leaned over to demonstrate. My lips almost touched the statue's cheek when her doubled fist smashed hard against my temple, knocking me back against the wall. The blow stunned me. She folded her arms and stood majestic, her smile suppressed behind wrinkled lips.

"Who do you think you are?" I shouted, struggling against humiliation and rage. "You think you own Christ. . . ."

I advanced toward her. She shook her finger slowly from side to side and stared me down.

"Only Judas kisses Christ's cheek in this season."

I looked at her dumbfounded as it became clear that she had saved me from being Judas. Gratitude replaced my anger.

"You are not Judas, I hope," she added.

"I hope not, too. Thank you for preventing me from acting like him."

"Kiss the body," she said, "but not the cheek."

Her triumph was total, but not unkind. She could afford to be magnanimous now that she had shown that a simple Tarascan peasant carried the Gospels in her very veins and heart and instincts as part of even her most spontaneous reactions, whereas the *gringo* outsider carried them only in his head and could forget them.

Moving into the compound where the crowd gathered, I approached the cell in which Christ was sequestered, ready to take photographs. Even though the guards had been told to cooperate with me, they reacted as guards might have in Christ's time, hoisting their spears menacingly.

I thought they were posing and prepared to shoot. When I brought the camera to my face, I felt the sharp end of the spear bruise hard into my abdomen. The crowd gasped as I bent double with pain. Recovering myself, I explained in whispers that I had Padre Tovar's permission to take photographs. Behind their red hoods I could detect neither consent nor understanding. I raised the camera again. A spear crashed into the lens guard, knocking it aside.

Again, through my anger, I realized they were living their roles. My permission to photograph them meant absolutely nothing.

The crowd, who hated the captors and guards of Christ, were with me. Once more I lifted the camera. The spear banged the side of my head. I reached up, grabbed the point and jerked it so hard the guard fell to the ground. I tossed the spear to one side, photographed the other guard and waited for the fallen one to get to his feet.

The crowd murmured approval as the faceless guard struggled to his feet and I stood my ground against him. But my sympathies were with him.

I was overwhelmed with my own sense of guilt at altering historical truth in this manner. Two thousand years ago no photographer had thus embarrassed Christ's guards. My actions distorted the truth of the day, changed it from what it should have been. The pain in my abdomen came from his attempt to right the distortion. I could only respect him for it. Disheartened, he retrieved his spear and resumed his stance as guard.

From across the silent compound our attention was drawn to a man's loud voice ordering guards to bring Christ to him. With a cynicism that chilled us, he added: "And don't fail to give the Master my distinguished regards." The centurion on horseback and foot guards approached the guarded door. They opened it and dragged out a haggard Christ, his face streaked with dried blood from the crown of thorns.

They shoved him toward the opposite side of the compound. There he was ordered stripped and flogged. The guards took him into the inside courtyard of the cloister, undressed him down to a white loincloth and whipped him relentlessly until every inch of his body trickled blood from the fine-line lash cuts. He received the blows in numbed silence.

When he was returned to the compound, the crowds cried for him to be crucified. Pilate argued with them, finding no fault with Christ. They demanded that Barabbas be set free and Christ killed. Pilate conceded, washing his hands, and turned the victim over to the mob. They clothed him in purple, slipping the silken garment over his body. Immediately the blood seeped through to darken the cloth.

With a heavy wooden cross loaded onto his shoulders, the young Tarascan Christ began his long walk through the olive trees toward Calvary. The crowd separated to let him pass. I waited in a good position to photograph him. When he approached, I stepped into the path and began walking backward in front of him. Barabbas, who gleefully preceded the Christ, swung his heavy chains hard against my legs. A guard knocked me off balance. When I stopped to rub my leg, Barabbas brought his chain down across my shoulders and neck.

As I photographed, Barabbas continued to chain whip me brutally across the back. Some of the crowd moved forward to defend me, but I waved them back. I concentrated away from the drubbing and photographed the Christ, his face hazed with pain in strange repose. I photographed the crowd of men and women, their eyes forlorn with tenderness and grief. Again, I burned with the embarrassment of my intrusion. Cameras did not belong in the Passion.

Christ fell faint in the red dust. I forgot myself, hurried to help him up, but was restrained by a spear in my belly. Intense silence surrounded all of this activity. The shepherd horn drifted over us from far away, accompanied by the savage thuds as the guards beat Christ until he staggered to his feet.

I knelt where I was, in his path, to get a close-up. The chains pounded against my back. I lost my balance and fell on my stomach. Christ was almost on me. His eyes were dazed. I froze, fearing he would stumble over me. I rolled on my back and reversed position, trying to move out his way. As his foot touched mine, he stopped. His glassy eyes cleared. He looked down at me patiently, intelligently, and with an expression of such sorrowful love that I felt devastated. Brutally, I reminded myself that this was not Christ, but a Tarascan youth playing a role. It did no good. The illusion was too powerful. During this instant of hesitation, I realized that my instincts as a photographer were functioning, that I was working the camera, photographing first his face and then his blood-blackened feet. Then I rolled to one side and out of the way, into the feet of the bystanders.

As he passed, the frightful stench of the dying Christ filled my nostrils, odors of sweat and souring blood. This too, I told myself, is how it must have been, with the dust, the stink, the dogs and chickens underfoot, the drink vendors, the women weeping, the men torn with pity, the children almost unconcerned, the total degradation of the God-Man. A weird implacable madness carried the scene forward in the slow rhythm of tragedy.

I filmed the almost nonchalant cruelty of scene after scene as the Christ fell and was flogged to his feet to continue and fall again. At one moment a piglet crossed his path. Then, when the Christ stood reeling, unable to take the next step, a hen came and pecked the dried blood on his feet, almost invisible in the red dust.

At the point where tensions could no longer be borne, an exquisite, white-clad Tarascan girl, representing the Virgin Mary, detached from the crowd and ran in a great floating motion toward the Christ. His eyes again cleared. He knelt on one knee and received her into his arms. She embraced the blood and stench. All action stopped. The madness vanished from the crowd. The gesture was so filled with tenderness that even the Christ's eyes filled with tears that diluted the blood on his cheeks. Barabbas stopped swinging his chain. Judas faded away into the crowd, his money bag jingling softly. Anger was defeated in us. Gently the guard pulled the Virgin Mary from the Christ's embrace. She was led away weeping while the Christ tottered forward. The crowd followed with dead hearts, obliged to go through the final portions of the walk to Calvary but wanting for it to be finished.

Again and again he fell. Again and again we heard the thuds. Again and again we felt the sickness of heart that must have been felt by those who witnessed it two thousand years ago. Our minds wandered. We became

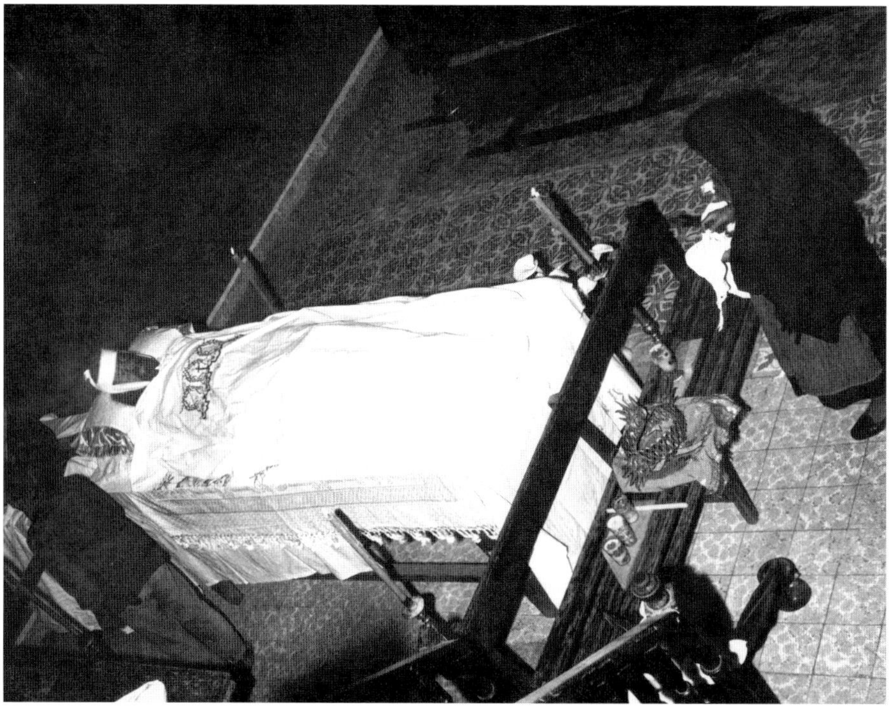

The young Tarascan who played the part of Christ during the Passion survived his ordeal, although nearly half of the men who play this role die, according to Padre Ernesto Tovar.

aware of the sun that blared down on our skulls, the dust that clogged our noses and dried our mouths, the hunger of the last hours, for the walk lasted until three in the afternoon when the Christ was pushed and shoved into the church.

At the rear of the deserted building where the altar had once been, the two crosses stood illuminated by a shaft of light from a window high in the wall. The Tarascan Christ had disappeared through a curtained doorway, and the life-sized *Cristo* was carried to the cross that lay flat on the floor. They hammered the *Cristo* to the cross with enormous brass nails. Then, while the crowd watched transfixed in grief, the huge cross was hoisted to an upright position with snow white ropes.

Muffled sobs threatened the silence. An elderly man walked into the sanctuary, knelt at the foot of the crosses, stared up at the *Cristo* figure and, with his arms outstretched in a gesture of abandon, began to intone a Tarascan chant, slow and flowing as an ocean wave. The silence was broken. The crowd knelt and joined their voices in the dirge.

The *Cristo* hung there dead before us. I slipped out the side door. The chant resounded through the countryside as I walked away. The crowd remained in the church to keep vigil. The late afternoon sun shone beautifully over the deserted compound turning purple bougainvillea blossoms transparent. Dust had settled. Vendors' stands were empty. Chickens pecked crumbs from the ground.

As I walked through the gate leading from the compound into the village, the messenger arrived from the hospital where they had rushed the young Tarascan Christ. He would live. He would be in the hospital three weeks, maybe four, but he would live.

The messenger rushed to spread the word throughout the church. Suddenly, as though on cue, roosters all over the valley began to crow.

I walked past olive trees pink-leaved from the dust, out onto the main street of the village. A young girl attended a stand where I bought a glass of lemonade. Neither of us spoke. The changes drifted to us muffled beneath the brilliant strider of the roosters' crowing. They would chant on through the night until the sounds of Easter and the mood of Resurrection were accomplished.

For this year, the Passion at Tzintzuntzan was over.

Young villagers in Tzintzuntzan, the morning after the Passion of Christ. This photograph first appeared in *Encounters With the Other: A Personal Journey* (1997).

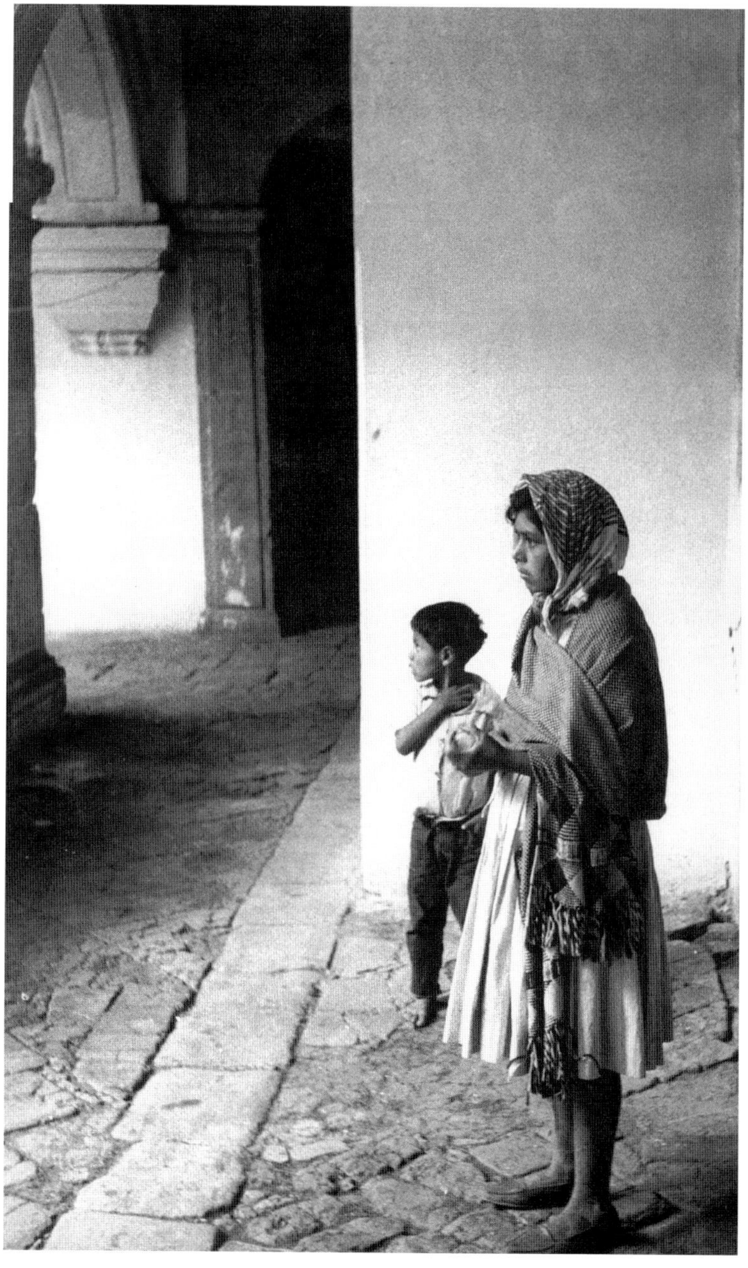

Notes on Photography

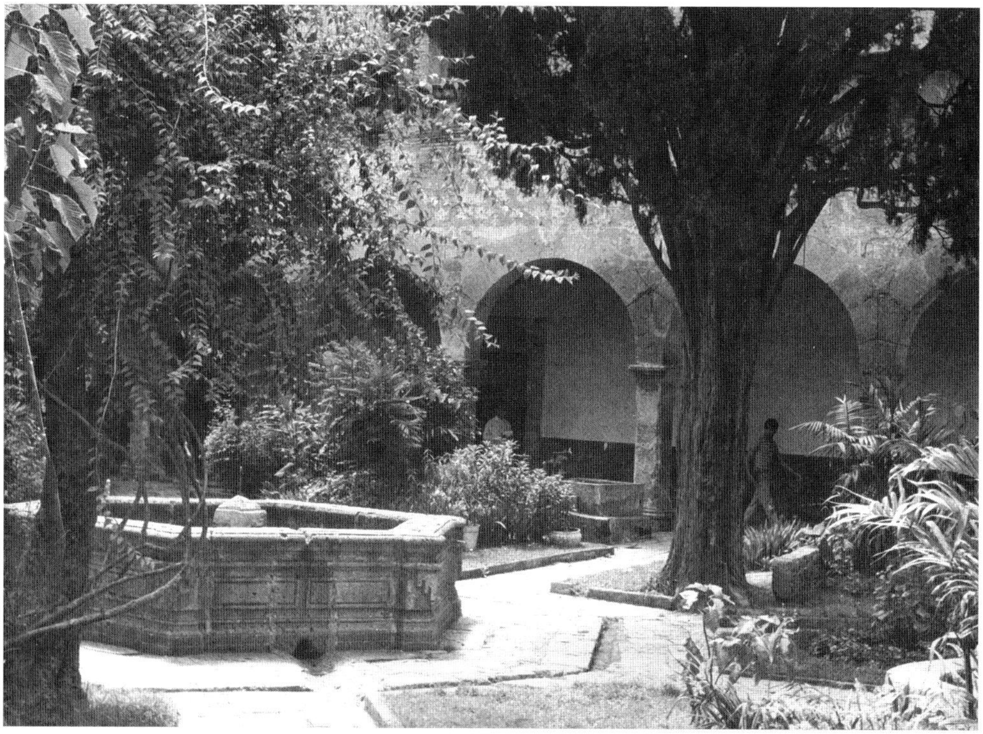

Courtyard of a school in Morelia, locally reputed to be the oldest school in the western hemisphere.

I.

It is another attempt, the same as writing, to penetrate the great welter of accidents that surround all objects and to get to the essences. I have no interest in the dramatic moment, but seek the moment that reveals the essential truths of an object or individual. This is not simple. It is a matter of struggling to perceive what might be, what is there to be discovered, of seeking, seeking always to get what is there. And it is a matter of accepting, too, the fact that one works with optics which see without partiality, sometimes cruelly what the eye, tied in with the whole affective nature, often sees differently.

There are no Dorian Grays where the fine lenses are concerned, and since I will never retouch, I destroy too-revealing negatives, ones that clearly reveal recesses for which the eye might compensate. To dredge men's recesses is not interesting. What is interesting is to find truths in them that can never be simulated – which means finally to find what is authentically human in the human visage.

II

Photography has exercised a long time compulsion in me, and I was becoming profoundly interested in certain aspects of photography – particularly those that opened possibilities to the same kind of thinking that my vocation as a novelist demanded – when I learned I was losing my sight.

In 1946, after the War, I was living in France, studying musicology and working in the great *Paléographie Musicale* at the Benedictine Abbey of Solesmes. I had very little vision left, and the possibilities of photography combining with the atmosphere of a beautiful rural community, dominated by a great monastery, intrigued me enormously. The tremendous rhythms of the monastic life, with their hours of silent labor and study interspersed with the ancient Gregorian Chants during the daily religious offices throughout the day somehow connected themselves to a spirit that could be dominant in photography – not the dramatic moment, but rather the typical moment, or the elevated moment (in a natural, not a bombastic sense).

Approaching blindness changes a man's view of things – he sees all things as miraculous, knowing he sees them for the last time, and this certainty that most people do not really see at all, or do not see into the essences of things, haunted me. I felt that if a novelist could put this kind of vision on paper, then a photographer could capture it. But obviously, photography and blindness are poor and torturous bedfellows; though the combination is possible. I began to devise ways of aiming my camera by sound (as I practiced throwing at sounds, shooting at sounds with a rifle), and found that with a little practice, one can achieve unerring aim.

But how to judge light? This, in brief, became easy. One learned the settings for a certain distance from the window on a bright or cloudy day, for instance.

When I had little vision left except light perception, I called on my neighbor in Solesmes, Pierre Reverdy, considered one of the greatest poets of his age. I began to experiment with a 35mm camera and the old Super-XX film. I judged from the sound of his voice the framing and distance, and then we talked until his tone indicated he had become more interested in our conversation than in posing for the camera.

When the roll was returned from a colleague who developed and printed for me, both he and Reverdy were quite excited. From the roll of twenty exposures, there were, they said, the finest portraits ever done of this artist. These were the ones used after that in all the newspaper and magazine stories about this famed poet.

I photographed sporadically during those years of blindness. But deprived of the ability to see the results of my work and to do the actual developing and printing, the process was too painful to sustain. Instead, I devoted myself entirely to writing books.

Then, when my sight was restored, I was in the midst of book commitments and did not return to photography until 1960. Of course, much of it was to be learned anew. I had some experience with photography, however, in doing assignments for magazines, and in being the subject of military magazine stories. Always the photographers who accompanied me on assignments, or who photographed me for articles, fascinated me.

Professional magazine photographers – for instance, Jim Hansen of *Look* or Shel Hershorn of *Life* or Mickey Pallas – taught me a great deal, simply by observing them in their work. Like most pros, they were enormously open and generous in telling me anything they could. However, the nagging desire to do my own photography, and in some way to combine it with my writing, would not leave me. Nor did I want to copy what others did.

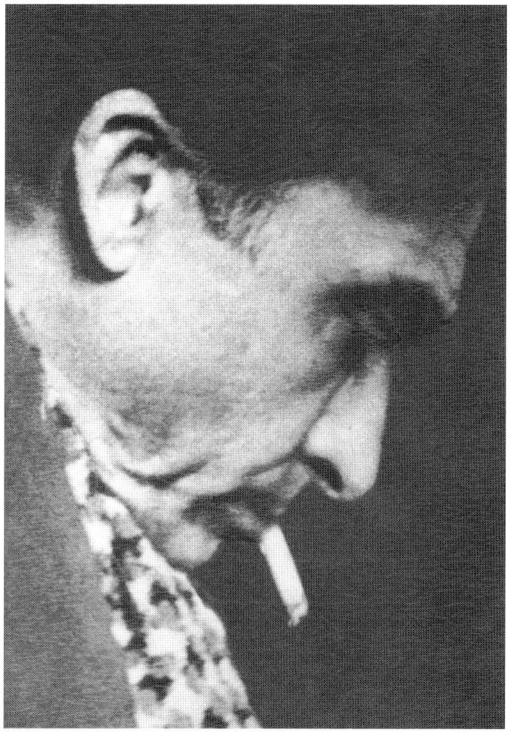

Griffin's portrait of the French poet, Pierre Reverdy, was taken in Solesmes, France, just before Griffin lost the last of his eyesight in 1946. The portrait was published on the covers of several of Reverdy's books, as well as in *The John Howard Griffin Reader.*

In France during the late-1930s, I had been a student at the Lycée Descartes, I had been much impressed by the spirit of Man Ray and others who were working experimentally. In those days, Eugène Atget had been forgotten, though his work was being preserved by that remarkable photographer, Berenice Abbot. I loved painting, and through this love I discovered that artists themselves were becoming excited about photography. I had occasion to see the portraits by men like Nadar and David Octavius Hill and was overwhelmed by them. There was no question of imitating painting, or even of comparing the two arts.

I wanted to see if my eye could capture the particular modality that had haunted me in my loss of sight, and again in my recovery of sight: to catch humanity not in its drama so much as its truth, its intelligence; to create works photographically that would reveal the compassion and inspiring qualities that all men, even the most degraded, radiate. Or perhaps more exactly to picture humanity in its mystery.

III

The opportunity to move to Mexico, to the beautiful city of Morelia in the State of Michoacán, confirmed me. We took my cameras, a basic darkroom set-up including a Leitz enlarger, and set out. We had taken a home on the mountain top in a little Tarascan village. It had been built two hundred years ago, and we began to have it reconditioned. But in the meantime we rented a home down the hill and fixed up a darkroom in the bathroom adjoining my studio.

It has been said that one cannot be a first-class photographer unless one does it full time. I had aims to become a first-class photographer and printer, and to retain a full writing schedule. In Mexico, where life is geared to a less hectic spirit, I found that it was possible to put in a full day of darkroom work and another full day of writing, without fatigue. I found Mexican photographers and printers equally hospitable, and learned how to purchase the best available photographic materials.

In Morelia, which has a decently-stocked Kodak store and another camera store handling Agfa materials, I experimented from four to eight hours a day in my darkroom, and frequently twelve or more hours. I obtained and used mostly Adox, Kodak and Agfa films and Agfa and Neffin developers. My Agfa dealer carried only Portrigo Rapido and Siltex in Agfa papers, and I quickly found these to be among the finest I could use. I developed a system of producing extremely sharp, thin negatives (usually with the slow emulsion Adox and Agfa films) and also for fast shooting, Plus-X (rated at 320 generally) and for super fast, Agfa Record, rated at ASA 2000.

The Tarascan country of Mexico (like most of Mexico) offers endless wealth to the photographer. I did not shoot promiscuously. I waited for the compelling subject, or the compelling moment in a given subject, or the peculiar combination of subject-surrounding-mood that would produce the feeling I was trying to capture – intelligence, serenity, communication of personality.

Also this was a matter of lighting, for I shot only available light and sought to twist composition from the clichés in a way that would increase the mood. I did many things that would horrify traditional photographers, and which in truth horrified me; but produced prints that eventually became traditional in their over-all effects.

If I sought light, composition, expression – nevertheless I was aiming at something else, something the novelist must deal with – expression of the basically inexpressible. In other words, a combination of elements that would produce the resonances in the viewer that I wanted him to have; works that would do something to the viewer rather than merely please his eye.

I realized that the photographer often errs when he photographs a thing that has great subjective importance, thinking it will strike the viewer with the same overtones. The point of challenge here was to analyze this, and to set about deliberately, with imagination and technique, to create the product that would involve the viewer. This is the novelist's constant challenge; it is the reason why the definition of art as "selectivity" is such a valid one.

In all such projects, the failures outweigh the successes. The temptation is to shout the point rather than whisper it. This ends up an obvious cliché, and will never wear well with the photographer even though he may have felt high enthusiasm for it initially. I think there is one basic truth about photography that has been said so often that it must be doubted. This is that the personal vision of the photographer can and does make the originality of his work.

If his vision is purely visual, then he can only produce images. If his vision is philosophical, then the work will take on a density of concept that opens the door to originality in the most banal shots.

He must develop taste, so that what he selects (from all the possible elements to photograph in a subject) creates the illusion of reality rather than merely the great clutter that is always involved in reality. He must go through great complexity, for every image, every communication is immensely complex, in order to arrive at simplicity – in order to make his vision speak in his own language.

The system I evolved, for better or worse, was something more than the "know your subject" one. I looked upon my neighbors, the Tarascans, and sought those elements in their culture that were universal to all men, and then sought those elements that were special to their ancient and beautiful culture: qualities of tenderness and dignity toward children; extreme fidelity to friendship; generosity and simplicity. And in the framework of the universal, to capture something of these other individualizing elements.

In all of this, printing techniques evolved of their own accord. I used most of the standard techniques – burning, dodging, ferracyniding; but rarely distortion, deliberate enlargement of grain or diffusion. In developing negatives, I was fortunate in that the water from our tap never varied from 68 degrees. I photographed with exact meter readings adapted to the points I wished to emphasize, with careful composition; and developed scrupulously by temperature and agitation, adapting these to the sort of negative I sought. On a role of 20 or 36 negatives, shot under diverse lighting conditions, the negatives would all have the same density. I also struggled to fill the frame exactly, so there would be as little cropping as possible. This gave negatives of sharpness, detail and fine-enough grain to take almost any blow-up desired.

I also figured my circle of confusion at 1/1500 inch instead of 1/750th. In other words, I estimated my depth of field two stops wider than the f stop I actually used (if f.11, I estimated depth of field for f. 5.6). However, I rarely shot with a hyperfocus technique, preferring to focus exactly on my subjects.

The Tarascans, until one knows them, are extremely reluctant to be photographed. In such instances, I found it easy to capture "unposed shots" by using a 35mm lens, setting it to hyperfocus (so that everything would be sharp from say six feet to infinity) and carrying the camera without a case at my side. A little practice enables you to maneuver into position, stare in the opposite direction and shoot the subject without his ever being aware that you were interested.

I shot several rolls of Plus-X one night on the island of Janitzio when I had used up all the available faster film. The scene was lighted by candles only, and though I was certain I would get nothing, I nevertheless shot the Plus-X, rating it at 250 and using a f.4 90mm lens. I developed them in the only developer available in the area (Agfa Atomal Neu), guessing at the time, since there was no green safelight for inspection. I got negatives that looked so thin I thought they would be good only for the waste basket.

To make matters worse, my stores carried nothing but normal #2 papers. I exposed rather heavy on the Agfa Portrigo (Artmatt) paper, developed quickly in undiluted Dektol, then rushed it into still cold water to let the details work in. Then put the almost flat prints (deep darks but weak highlights) into the fixer and began the torturous job of bringing up the highlights with weak ferracynide. I ended up with extraordinarily beautiful 11 x 14s, sharp and fine-grained with Plus-X, and far less beautiful ones with the high speed negatives.

The photographer's work must express what he wants to express, it must be deliberate and he must choose the means of making it so. He must master the art of developing and printing, which are highly individual techniques which no one else can do for him in order to bring out exactly his vision. He must feel, after mastery of technique is out of the way, a continuously greater freedom to stretch his medium and his belief in its capabilities.

– Mexico, 1960

Donkeys on the road leading out of the ancient city of Tzintzuntzan. This photograph was first published in *Encounters with the Other: A Personal Journey.*

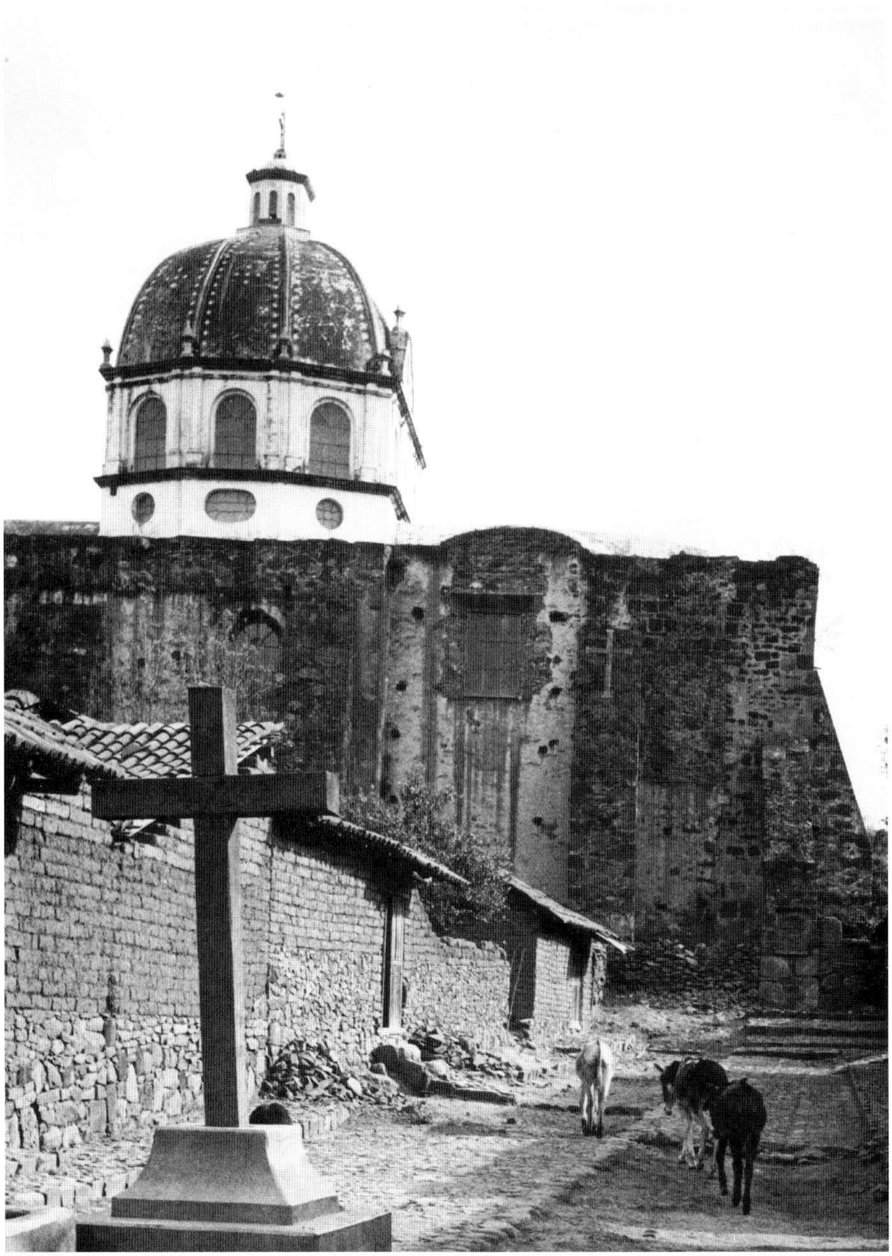

Later Reflections

As music demands cooperation and even participation of the listener, so photography demands them of the viewer. If the viewer does not project himself into a photograph enough to smell the odors, hear the sounds and silences, feel the permeation of atmosphere or mood, then he is not looking correctly. This cannot be done by glancing. It takes time. The viewer must, in a sense, give himself up to the photograph, let it take him where it will. Many viewers look searchingly only at photographs of themselves.

The allusion to music has some validity. Both, if they are worthy, must strike universal resonances in a wide variety of people. To listen only to the melodic line of a Bach fugal theme and fail to hear the counterpoint and harmony, or perceive the structure, is similar to seeing only what is superficially obvious in a photograph. In his *Daybooks,* Edward Weston said he judged the success of his photographs in accordance with their visual resemblance to Bach fugues.

But all of these evocations must be implicit in the photograph. This is the photographer's frustration. How to get them onto the negative and then how to make the negatives come to life in the darkroom.

Nell Dorr, in her magnificent photographic study of Teotitlan del Valle, *The Bare Feet,* wrote: "Now I am at home in the quiet of my darkroom. The door to the outside is closed and only my pictures are with me. Once again, my old fear returns to haunt me: Will they breathe?"

Will they breathe? Will it all be there when the prints begin to form under an amber safelight in the developing solution? The darkroom is a place of tension at such moments as the photographer studies the emerging print and wonders if he has fulfilled in it the vision he had when he clicked the shutter of his camera. Has he sufficiently emphasized the important areas, obscured the unimportant ones, coaxed out a proper gradation of tones?

Marion Palfi's photographic essays communicate these evocations in an almost transforming manner – particularly in her geriatrics series, *You Have*

Never Been Old, where the viewer is taken so profoundly into the life and problems of the aged.

At Aspen I photographed the Amadeus Quartet playing Schubert. But I failed somehow because the final prints evoked no sound. My photos were an injustice to the performers who appeared to play on silent instruments.

In Minneapolis I photographed Zara Nelsova performing a Bach partita for unaccompanied cello. This was better in that something of the music came through in the composition, the tonality and the expression on the artist's face.

These things may well come to life for the photographer in his prints, but he must wonder how many viewers will see, hear, smell and experience fully what is really there.

– *Journal*, May 5, 1966

Portrait of Zara Nelsova, the world-renowned cellist, performing in 1963 in Minneapolis. This portrait appeared in *The John Howard Griffin Reader.*

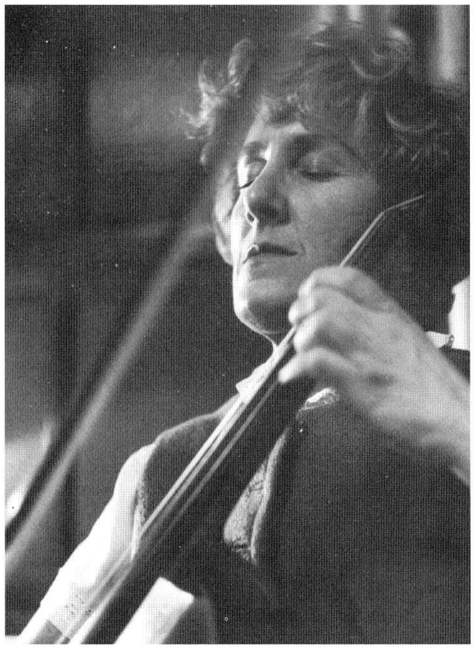

Notes and Acknowledgments

Rights to Griffin's works are held by The Estate of John Howard Griffin and Elizabeth Griffin-Bonazzi. Acknowledgments are due to Estate members, the children of Elizabeth and John Howard Griffin: Susan Griffin-Campbell, John Griffin, Gregory Parker Griffin and Amada Griffin-Fenton, to whom this book is dedicated.

The original typescript of "Notes on Photography" was drafted in 1960 during Griffin's exile in Mexico (Parts II and III appear in print for the first time). Parts I and IV are adapted from the photographic section of *The John Howard Griffin Reader* (edited by Bradford Daniel, Houghton Mifflin 1968).

"The Watch of the Dead" was written in 1960 and first published in *Encounters With the Other: A Personal Journey* (edited by Robert Bonazzi, Latitudes 1997).

"Passion at Tzintzuntzan" was written in 1961 and first published in *The John Howard Griffin Reader;* it was reprinted in *Encounters With the Other: A Personal Journey.*

The passages from Griffin's *Journal* and his letters quoted in the "Introduction" are published here for the first time. His friends' letters are quoted with permission.

Griffin works cited in "Introduction" are: three novels, *The Devil Rides Outside* (Smiths 1952, William Collins 1953, Pocketbooks 1954), *Nuni* (Houghton Mifflin 1956) and *Street of the Seven Angels* (Wings 2003); three nonfiction titles, *Black Like Me* (Wings, Estate Edition, Indexed, 2006), *Scattered Shadows: A Memoir of Blindness and Vision* (Orbis 2004) and *Land of the High Sky,* a history of the Staked Plains Region of West Texas (First National Bank of Midland 1959).

Many of the photographs from Mexico appear for the first time in *Available Light.* Those previously published are credited in the captions to those photographs. Griffin's portraits of Jacques Maritain, Father Stanley Murphy, Edgar Griffin and Decherd Turner were made after the exile in Mexico.

Thanks to Kathy Vargas, Bryce Milligan and Dan Robertson for their astute insights.

John Howard Griffin, Photographer

John Howard Griffin's (1920-1980) fascination with photography began when he was a student in France in the late 1930s, but he was unable to perfect his knowledge of the topic for many years. As a member of the French Underground, he was forced to flee from a Gestapo death squad in 1940. He returned to the States and joined the Army Air Force, serving in the South Pacific for three years, where he was wounded in a Japanese air raid. A severe concussion, combined with undetected diabetes, led to the progressive loss of his eyesight. He returned to France in 1946, where he studied Gregorian Chant with the Benedictines in their monastery at Solesmes, and took his first important photographs – portraits of French poet Pierre Reverdy, which appeared in several European magazines and on the covers of Reverdy's books. Finally, completely blind, Griffin returned to Texas, turning his full attention to writing. He completed his three novels, over fifty short stories, and began keeping his *Journal* during a decade of blindness. He regained his sight in January of 1957. This remarkable story can be read in his powerful *Scattered Shadows: A Memoir of Blindness and Vision.*

In the fall of 1959, Griffin made his historic journey through the Deep South disguised as a Negro. *Available Light* begins after the events of *Black Like Me* as he, his young family and elderly parents are moving to Mexico in 1960 – driven out of Mansfield by death threats from local racists. Griffin began again to experiment with photography after regaining sight, but it was not until the exile in Mexico that he became a serious artist. He produced an unpublished folio of matted prints, *Return of the Spirit,* with hand-printed commentary, his first attempt to combine photography and writing. The story of Griffin's time in Mexico, when he actually wrote the book version of *Black Like Me* and was immersed in photography, has been little-known. Yet it was a significant period in his growth as a visual artist, and it was a brief retreat from the pressures of public controversy that would change his life drastically with the publication of *Black Like Me.*

In a *Journal* entry for June 3, 1963, Griffin wrote: "I note that nothing really interests me in photography except human faces." During the 1960s and 70s, he made portraits of important 20th century figures in philosophy, social justice, literature and the arts: Thomas Merton, Jacques Maritain, Artur Rubinstein, Roland Hayes, Lili Kraus, Dominique Pire, Bede Griffiths, Viktor Frankel, Mark Van Doren, Denise Levertov, Dick Gregory, Saul Alinsky, Daniel Berrigan, Alicia de Larrocha, Abraham Rattner, Josh White, Arthur Lourié, Robert Casadesus, Jean Casadesus, Andrew Dasburg, Nell Dorr, Archie Moore, Zara Nelsova, John Jacob Niles, Maxwell Geismar, Michael Tippit, James Laughlin, Jonathan Kozol, Elena Costa, John Reeves, Truman Nelson, Annie Fischer, P.D. East, Sarah Patton Boyle, John Beecher, Penn Jones, Luiz Carlos Moura-Castro, Bridget Moura-Castro, G. Curtsinger, and many others.

While his portraits appeared widely in periodicals and on book covers, it was not until the photographic folio included in *The John Howard Griffin Reader* (1968) that his magnificent portraiture began to be appreciated internationally as art. He followed with the masterful art book, *A Hidden Wholeness: The Visual World of Thomas Merton* (1970), featuring Griffin's commentary on Merton's art and photography, as well as his authorized portraits of the monk and his hermitage. Later titles included *Twelve Photographic Portraits* in 1973 and a book about his mentor: *Jacques Maritain: Homage in Words and Pictures* in 1974. Griffin held memberships in both the American Society of Magazine Photographers and the Royal Photographic Society of Great Britain – one of the few individuals to belong to both organizations.

Griffin's massive archive of original prints and negatives remain the property of The Estate of John Howard Griffin and his literary papers reside in various university collections.

About Robert Bonazzi

Robert Bonazzi first interviewed John Howard Griffin for *Latitudes* magazine in 1966. Beginning in the late 1960s, his essays on Griffin's life and work were published in *The New York Times, Village Voice, National Catholic Reporter, Bloomsbury Review, Motive, Southwest Review, Texas Observer, New Orleans Review* and in compendiums about African-Americans, including *The Historical Dictionary of Civil Rights.*

He was named "Authorized Biographer" by the Griffin Estate in 1983, and wrote an afterword to the 35th anniversary edition of *Black Like Me* (Penguin, 1996). In 1997, Orbis Books published his critically-acclaimed *Man in the Mirror: John Howard Griffin and the Story of Black Like Me.* That same year, Griffin's *Encounters With the Other: A Personal Journey,* including unpublished writings and photographs, was published by Latitudes Press.

As Literary Executor for the Estate, Bonazzi has edited the following books by Griffin for Wings Press: *Street of the Seven Angels* (novel, 2003); the Griffin Estate edition of *Black Like Me* 2004; updated and indexed in 2006); and *Available Light: Exile in Mexico* (2008). For Orbis Books, he edited *Follow the Ecstasy: The Hermitage Years of Thomas Merton* (1993) and *Scattered Shadows: A Memoir of Blindness and Vision* (2004).

His books of poetry and poetics include *Maestro of Solitude* (Wings 2007), *Perpetual Texts* (Latitudes 1986), *Fictive Music* (Wings 1979) and *Living the Borrowed Life* (New Rivers 1974). His work has appeared in over 200 publications in France, Germany, Japan, Canada, Mexico, Peru, the UK and the US. Bonazzi's Latitudes Press (1966-2000) published 112 literary titles, including international writers in English and translation.

About Kathy Vargas

Kathy Vargas is an internationally praised artist/photographer whose exhibitions include one-person shows at Sala Uno in Rome and the Galeria San Martín in Mexico City. A retrospective was mounted in 2000 by the McNay Museum in San Antonio, Texas. Her work was featured in "Hospice: A Photographic Inquiry" for the Corcoran gallery and "Chicano Art: Resistance and Affirmation (CARA)." Works by Vargas hang in numerous museums, including the Smithsonian American Art Museum. She was the director of the visual arts program at the Guadalupe Cultural Arts Center for many years. She currently is the Chair of the Art and Music Department at the University of the Incarnate Word in San Antonio, Texas, her hometown. In 2005, Vargas was named "Texas State Two-Dimensional Artist," the visual artist's equivalent of Poet Laureate.

Colophon

This first edition of *Available Light: Exile in Mexico,* by John Howard Griffin, has been printed on 70 pound non-acidic paper containing fifty percent recycled fiber. Titles and inital capitals have been set using Colonna type, text in Caslon, and captions in Tahoma. This volume was edited by Robert Bonazzi. Wings Press books are designed by Bryce Milligan.

Wings Press was founded in 1975 by Joanie Whitebird and Joseph F. Lomax, both deceased, as "an informal association of artists and cultural mythologists dedicated to the preservation of the literature of the nation of Texas." The publisher/editor since 1995, Bryce Milligan is honored to carry on and expand that mission to include the finest in American writing, without commercial considerations clouding the choice to publish or not to publish. Wings Press attempts to produce multicultural books, chapbooks, CDs, DVDs and broadsides that, we hope, enlighten the human spirit and enliven the mind. We at Wings know well that writing is a transformational art form capable of changing the world, primarily by allowing us to glimpse something of each other's souls. Good writing is innovative, insightful, and interesting. But most of all it is honest.

Wings Press
www.wingspress.com
Distributed to the trade by the Independent Publishers Group
www.ipgbook.com